Mystic Chords of Memory

Mystic Chords of
CIVIL WAR BATTLEFIELDS

Memory

AND HISTORIC SITES RECAPTURED

Photographs and Text by David J. Eicher

Foreword by John Y. Simon

LOUISIANA STATE UNIVERSITY PRESS

Baton Rouge

Copyright © 1998 by Louisiana State University Press

All rights reserved

Manufactured in China

First printing

07 06 05 04 03 02 01 00 99 98   5 4 3 2 1

Designer: Laura Roubique Gleason
Typeface: Granjon
Printer and binder: Everbest Printing Co. through Four Colour Imports, Ltd., Louiville, Kentucky

Library of Congress Cataloging-in-Publication Data:

Eicher, David J., 1961–

    Mystic chords of memory : Civil War battlefields and historic sites
recaptured / photographs and text by David J. Eicher.

       p.   cm.

    Includes bibliographical references and index.

    ISBN 0-8071-2309-9 (cloth : alk. paper)

    1. United States—History—Civil War, 1861–1865—Battlefields—Pictorial
works.   2. United States—History—Civil War, 1861–1865—Monuments—
Pictorial works.   3. Historic sites—United States—Pictorial works.   I. Title.

E468.7.E38   1998

973.7'6—dc21   98-20247
CIP

For Lynda, who,
when discussing vacation plans, has come to tolerate
hearing, "How about Gettysburg?"

CONTENTS

FOREWORD

At the start of each new year I face the same problem. It's time to hang the latest edition of David Eicher's splendid *Civil War Journeys* calendar. What should I do with the old one? Simply pitching last year's calendar means never again seeing a superb array of evocative photographs of Civil War sites; saving the old calendar brands me as compulsive. Each year I have decided to put it aside, believing that I can throw it out later, when I will miss the photographs less. I haven't got around to this yet; now I can. Eicher has created a book blending choice photographs with an engaging narrative of the conflict.

The son of a professor of organic chemistry at Miami University, Eicher developed a precocious interest in science, especially astronomy, that led him at age sixteen to launch a newsletter for amateur astronomers. After attending Miami University, he joined the staff of *Astronomy* magazine, where he has ascended to managing editor. Widely published in the field of astronomy, Eicher decided to pursue another intellectual enthusiasm as well.

For the past decade, Dave and his father have annually traveled to Civil War battlefields, developing a family interest shared eventually by his sister Nancy. Dave has already photographed some 10,000 Civil War scenes. Besides his own splendid calendar, this collection has provided illustrations for numerous books and magazines. Eicher's other Civil War interests have already resulted in *Civil War Battlefields: A Touring Guide* (1995); an immense bibliographical survey, *The Civil War in Books* (1996); and an iconographic study, *Robert E. Lee: A Life Portrait* (1997). Contemplated Eicher books include a photographic study of Ulysses S. Grant and another of Gettysburg. Great-great-grandson of a private of the 74th Ohio, Dave seemingly has a mystical connection to the past at Civil War sites that animates his photographs. None represents mere scenery.

Eicher's photographs capture the terrible beauty of the contemporary Civil War monuments and battlefields. Banal American names like Gettysburg and Vicksburg have acquired singular resonance, while others, like Shiloh, Chickamauga, and Appomattox, vibrate magically. Each field commemorates both gallantry and savagery, heroism and cowardice, victory and defeat, death and rebirth. From the slaughter of thousands arose a new United States of America. An idealistic society, yet one that sheltered the institution of slavery, achieved redemption through bloody struggle. Few foresaw war's dire consequences. None could anticipate the magnitude of the struggle.

Immediately after the battle of Gettysburg, while dead horses still littered the ground, officials began to plan a national cemetery, a site for quiet, neat, respectful, orderly consecration of a portion of the field. Lincoln's dedicatory speech, delivered more than four months later, the product of careful thought and revision, avoided references to Union triumph and emphasized national principle. The Gettysburg Address joined the titanic struggle in hallowing that field.

In the summer of 1865, journalist John T. Trowbridge left Boston to tour Civil War battlefields. A thirty-eight-year-old abolitionist with no firsthand experience of war, Trowbridge visited places retaining remnants of carnage and horror. Trees blasted by firepower were called "deadenings." Impoverished southerners wandered the fields searching for lead and marketable clothing. One guide boasted of trading a dead man's blanket for a half bushel of meal. Plowmen disturbed the hasty and shallow burials of wartime. At Chickamauga, troops still sought bodies of the fallen. For nearly a generation, most combat veterans found these battlefields too painful to visit.

After time reclaimed and softened these fields, the passion to memorialize spawned forests of monuments and markers throughout land eventually sanctified as National Battlefield Parks. Visiting these sites, survivors were sometimes moved to tears. Ceremonies of reconciliation attracted veterans of both sides to fields including Gettysburg, where reunion occasionally gave way to reawakened memories of old antagonisms. The last of these reunions occurred in 1938, the seventy-fifth anniversary of the battle.

Battlefields were eventually landscaped to provide an interpretation of the conflict. New Deal projects restored some eroded trenches and earthworks. Neatly mowed grass marked the arrival of the National Park Service. Often the fields of death resembled picnic grounds.

Some photographers have gone to great lengths to avoid including statues and monuments in contemporary battlefield landscapes. Eicher recognizes that forests of stone and marble, heartfelt tributes of survivors, have their own role on the field.

In March 1864, Lieutenant General Ulysses S. Grant, recently invested with command of all the armies of the United States, turned down an invitation to dine at the White House with President Abraham Lincoln. "I have become very tired of this show business," he explained. Show business has always been an important component of military life. Troops in formation, officers grandly caparisoned, polished weapons, bugles and drums, flags and banners, all constitute part of the pageantry of war. Spotting the headquarters banner of General George Meade, a golden eagle in a silver wreath, Grant asked if Imperial Caesar were nearby. Yet Grant himself had carefully donned full uniform before first leading the Army of the Potomac into battle.

Within a year, General Robert E. Lee wore his most elegant uniform and carried a jeweled sword to surrender to Grant at the McLean House at Appomattox Court House. Cut off from his headquarters, Grant appeared in muddy boots and ordinary uniform for the ceremony, transformed into a tableau of reunion. In the 1950s, the National Park Service reconstructed the McLean House with careful attention to detail. The symbolic beauty of the occasion deserved no less.

Whether viewed as fields of death or fields of glory—and they were both—Civil War sites retain a powerful hold on the American imagination. In words as well as photographs, Eicher captures the drama of America's greatest conflict.

John Y. Simon

PREFACE

*T*he "mystic chords of memory" Lincoln spoke of at his first inauguration (see chapter 1) apply not just to the American scene of 1861. Indeed, the mystic chords seem to stretch across the generations from the Civil War era to the present, bonding modern Americans to the nation's most traumatic and defining event. In the last few years, millions watched and were moved by Ken Burns's *The Civil War* on PBS television. Millions of others have been inspired by the motion pictures *Glory* and *Gettysburg,* and the active interest of Civil War history is booming today like it never has before—not even during the heyday of the Centennial years in the 1960s. Many still treasure the relics and papers of ancestors who fought in the war. Still others gather at round tables each month to refight the war in their discussions, and many others don uniforms for the growing numbers of reenactments.

I was caught up in the current fever of Civil War history after being given papers and mementos of my great-great-grandfather, Pvt. Darius Wetzel of the 74th Ohio Infantry, who survived the war and lived until 1903. Among the items was a soapstone "bible" carved by Wetzel, bearing his wife's initials, which he carried through Sherman's March to the Sea. He also came into possession of a Remington New Army model 1858 pistol, burned on the battlefield of Antietam and picked up shortly afterward. The wooden grips were long gone and two of the chambers clogged with rust. Many years later, in the late 1930s, my grandfather set out to clean the gun. He placed the cylinder on a stake and built a bonfire around it. Sure enough, after a couple of minutes, the family heard "bang!" "bang!"—the two bullets remaining in the cylinder exploded. (No one was injured.) So, as my grandmother liked to say, "the last two shots of the Civil War were fired in Dayton, Ohio."

In one sense the war seems incredibly distant, and yet it was fought less than two lifetimes ago. Indeed, my grandmother as a young girl fetched an occasional bucket of beer for the aged veteran Wetzel—her grandfather—who sat on their Ohio porch. When asked such questions as "Did you really accompany General Sherman through Georgia?" Wetzel allegedly said, with mock crankiness and apparent truth, "Hell no—I marched ahead of Sherman and built the bridges he crossed over."

Such personal connections to momentous events strengthen the bonds we feel most strongly when visiting the sites where Civil War actions occurred. I began photographing Civil War battlefields and other historic sites in the mid-1980s after my father and I began a series of annual trips to all of the important places associated with the war we could find. I wanted to see what remained of the war today—what one could really see of the famous places known so well by the soldiers and civilians of the war era. I began publishing these images in the annual *Civil War Journeys* wall calendar, produced by Tide-mark Press, East Hartford, Connecticut, since 1990. Continuing my journeys to the war, I've now amassed a collection of more than 10,000 such images, and I have presented a selection of the best in this volume.

If this project has a godfather, it surely must be John Y. Simon, editor of *The Papers of Ulysses S. Grant* and a good friend. John's enthusiasm over the photographs and encouragement to publish them as a book have spurred me into action on many late nights. I owe him a great debt for his kind willingness to contribute a foreword to this volume. As always, I must thank my father John, who got me into Civil War history to begin with, and who is an expert historian of the war. Our ongoing adventures on the road in both overcrowded cities and virtually deserted countryside constitute some of my fondest memories. For their continued encouragement on a variety of projects, and for unselfish contribution of their time, I wish to thank Gary Gallagher and Jim McPherson. I also wish to thank Sylvia Frank of Louisiana State University Press for her enthusiasm over this project, and for the opportunity to join the distinguished ranks of LSU authors in Civil War history. My thanks also to my editor at LSU, Gerry Anders, whose expert editing and advice made this book a sharper product.

Finally, I owe my deepest gratitude to my wife Lynda and son Chris, who during too many hours need to share father with ghosts from the past.

Dave Eicher

Mystic Chords of Memory

STORM CLOUDS ON THE HORIZON

*I*t was the dawn of a new age for Washington City. As the morning began it seemed that spring was in the air, though the weather would later chill the throngs gathered to see the new leader inaugurated. On March 4, 1861, the focal point of the American nation was Abraham Lincoln, who only a few months earlier would have seemed an unlikely person to play the leading role in the great drama unfolding in the capital's streets. Some 25,000 visitors mingled with the city's 61,000 residents to witness Lincoln's taking the oath as the nation's sixteenth president. Security was a major concern: regular army squads armed with rifles stood on rooftops along Pennsylvania Avenue with orders to shoot anyone wielding a weapon from a window on the opposite side of the street. No such violence came. The nation, however, would not cooperate as well as the local crowds. The United States was coming apart at its center, verging on a rebellion that had nearly come during a succession of crises dating back to Andrew Jackson's tenure in the Executive Mansion.

The eastern royalty of American politics watched and listened as Lincoln—the tall, gaunt westerner whom most of them considered a hayseed—took on a greater challenge than that accepted by George Washington on the eve of the nation's first administration. Lincoln made a plea to the distraught southern states that had seceded or threatened to secede from the Union. "We are not enemies, but friends," he said. In his new tall hat and black suit, the newly inaugurated leader delivered a stirring speech—"as if he had been delivering inaugural addresses all his life," according to Henry Watterson, a Tennessee journalist who would edit several Confederate newspapers during the war.[1]

Lincoln concluded with a near-poetic appeal: "The mystic chords of memory, stretching from every battle-field, and patriot grave, to every living heart and hearthstone, all over this broad land, will yet swell the chorus of the Union, when again touched, as surely they will be, by the better angels of our nature." Wilder Dwight, a future Union officer, was there. "When the address closed and the cheering subsided, Taney rose," wrote Dwight, referring to Roger Brooke Taney, the pro-southern chief justice of the Supreme Court. "And, almost as tall as Lincoln, he administered the oath, Lincoln repeating it; and as the words, 'preserve, protect, and defend the Constitution' came ringing out, he bent and kissed the book; and for one, I breathed freer and gladder than for months. The man looked a man, and acted a man and a president."[2]

The United States had a new administration, with Hannibal Hamlin of Maine serving as Lincoln's vice president. For the South, this new leadership represented the latest in a series of events that was too much to bear. The South had lost power in national politics after a heritage of controlling most events; it viewed the "black Republican" Lincoln as a direct threat to the economic interest of slavery, to self-determination, and to the southern lifestyle itself.

Abraham and Mary Lincoln Home, Springfield, Illinois

In 1837 Lincoln moved to Springfield, five years later marrying Mary Todd, a fellow Kentuckian. In 1843 the Lincolns bought the only house they ever owned, at Eighth and Jackson Streets, for $1,200 cash and a small lot worth $300. Here they lived until 1861.

The roots of the war ran deep. For years the North and South had been evolving in different directions. The southern agrarian economy, based in large part on plantation farming supported by slave labor, stood in sharp contrast to the emerging industrialization and accelerating flow of immigrant free labor into the North. The two sections were in fact like sister countries bound by an economic tryst. The 1850s proved pivotal for both. The nation's population increased by 35 percent. The land's wealth of resources began to be tapped in force, including brisk trading in wood, coal, copper, and gold. Production of food skyrocketed. Railroads threaded across the landscape, the total mileage of track reaching more than 30,000. All this growth and prosperity brought decisions as well, none more crucial than when Kansas and Nebraska approached statehood and the potential legality of slavery in new states and territories became a hot political issue.

A polarizing event occurred on May 30, 1854, when the Kansas-Nebraska Act, authored by Senator Stephen A. Douglas of Illinois, was passed by Congress. The act allowed admittance into the Union of future states with constitutions that provided for slavery; it thus upheld the notion of popular sovereignty, while forgoing the use of federal laws to restrict slavery's spread. It destroyed the tenuous balance of power that had existed previously and set up a violent border war of guerrilla-style skirmishes between Free-Soilers and proslavery men in the western territories.

Four years later Lincoln, a Springfield, Illinois, attorney whose scant national renown came from a single congressional term in the 1840s, violently attacked popular sovereignty and slaveholding interests. Before a packed house in the state capitol in Springfield on June 16, 1858, Lincoln told his fellow politicians: "A house divided against itself cannot stand. I believe this government cannot endure

Lincoln-Herndon Law Office and Old State Capitol, Springfield, Illinois

From Lincoln's law office, shared with partner William H. Herndon, the rising politician could look out his window onto the State Capitol dome. Lincoln gave his "house divided" speech in the capitol in 1858.

Thomas Lincoln Cabin, Hodgenville, Kentucky

On February 12, 1809, Abraham Lincoln was born in a log cabin in the Kentucky wilderness. The cabin preserved now allegedly contains at least portions of the original structure.

Harpers Ferry photographed by James Gardner in July 1865. Note the ruins of the U.S. Arsenal-Armory at center and left of center.

Harpers Ferry, West Virginia

In October 1859 Harpers Ferry—at the time part of Virginia—saw an abortive raid by the fanatical abolitionist John Brown, who attempted to capture arms and spark a slave rebellion.

permanently half slave and half free. I do not expect the Union to be dissolved—I do not expect the house to fall—but I do expect it will cease to be divided. It will become all one thing, or all the other."[3]

Such words fueled the fear of southern politicians and their constituents. But nothing fired political passions like the bungled attack by the fanatical abolitionist

John Brown on the U.S. Arsenal-Armory at Harpers Ferry, Virginia. A veteran of the Kansas-Nebraska border wars, Brown led twenty-one antislavery zealots (including five black Americans) armed with pikes and muskets to the Booth Kennedy farmhouse in Dargan, Maryland, where they plotted their strike on Harpers Ferry. They planned to capture arms, spread them to local slaves, and incite a regional rebellion that would liberate tens of thousands and effectively end slavery in America.

Jefferson's Rock, Harpers Ferry

Overlooking the confluence of the Potomac and Shenandoah Rivers, Jefferson's Rock offers a view that Thomas Jefferson proclaimed "worthy of a voyage across the Atlantic."

Carried out on October 16, 1859, the raid failed miserably. Holed up in the arsenal's enginehouse, the group was surrounded by a mixed force of U.S. infantry, marines, and local militia led by Brevet Colonel Robert E. Lee, who had been summoned from staff duty to put down the insurgency. Lee, born to a distinguished family of Virginia's aristocracy, originated from a different world than that of the rough westerners who would take over the government in Washington fifteen months hence. His father, although later falling from grace, had been governor of the Commonwealth. Lee's career as an engineer in the U.S. Army had been outstanding, his service in the Mexican War stellar. His loyalty to the U.S. Army never had faltered, but soon he would face the dilemma created by Virginia's departure from the Union.

For now, however, Lee—aided by Lieutenant James E. B. Stuart—surrounded the enginehouse and captured ten of Brown's raiders, including Brown himself. Seven of the party were killed during the fiasco. The event sent shock waves through the South. After a brief trial, Brown was hanged in Charles Town on December 2. Before his death, the self-proclaimed agent of God handed a note to the executioner that read, "I John Brown am now quite certain that the crimes of this guilty, land: will never be purged away; but with Blood."[4]

Stratford Hall Plantation, Stratford, Virginia

Robert E. Lee was born at Stratford, in Westmoreland County, Virginia, on January 19, 1807. The Lees soon moved to Alexandria.

**Dr. Booth Kennedy Farmhouse,
Dargan, Maryland**

*In the summer of 1859 John Brown rented this house,
recruited an "army" of twenty-one men, and planned
an act that, he hoped, would alter world history.*

**U.S. Arsenal-Armory Enginehouse,
Harpers Ferry**

*John Brown's raid ended in this building, sometimes
called "John Brown's Fort," where he and most of his
men were cornered and captured. The building has
been moved slightly from the original site.*

Battery Park Houses, Charleston, South Carolina

The gathering clouds of war thickened following Lincoln's election. Southerners, particularly South Carolinians, saw the result as an affront to their society and lifestyle, symbolized by the beautiful row houses along Charleston's Battery Park.

Brown proved to be prescient in death. A year later the tensions between North and South were palpable, the deep southern states—particularly the hotbed of secession, South Carolina—on the verge of withdrawing from the country. "Prevent, as far as possible, any of our friends from demoralizing themselves and our cause by entertaining propositions for compromise of any sort on 'slavery extension,'" Lincoln wrote his friend Elihu B. Washburne on December 13, 1860. "On that point hold firm, as with a chain of steel."[5]

But South Carolinians held firm as well. Citizens in Charleston, the most fervent secessionist city, emphasized their contempt for the Union by wearing cockades of palmetto fronds, the South Carolina state symbol. Southrons assembled in droves in the city in December and held a secession convention. All the state's prominent politicians attended, along with many dignitaries from surrounding states. Secession seemed a foregone conclusion, although new laws to govern the state would have to be enacted and ways found to handle tasks previously done by the federal government. Finally, on December 20, the convention voted for an ordinance of secession. "We . . . the people of South Carolina," it read, "have solemnly declared that the Union heretofore existing between this State and the other States of North America is dissolved, and that the State of South Carolina has resumed her position among the nations of the world, as a separate and independent state." Not all Charlestonians approved of the action. James Louis Petigru, a prominent attorney and statesman, said that South Carolina was too small to be a nation and too large for an insane asylum.[6]

But the deed was done. In the South, the Union was dissolving. In the North, agitated citizens expected the government to do something about southern secession. President Buchanan acted by doing nothing at all. "We are divorced, North

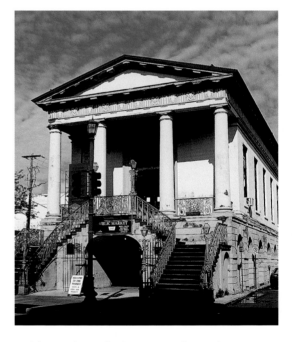

Public Market, Charleston, South Carolina

Citizens of Charleston gathered daily at the city's social epicenter, the Public Market, to discuss their state's secession and the looming threat of war.

and South," wrote the Charleston diarist Mary Boykin Chesnut, "because we have hated each other so."[7] Other southern states followed South Carolina's lead: Mississippi seceded on January 9, 1861; Florida the following day; Alabama on January 11; Georgia on the nineteenth; Louisiana a week later; Texas on February 1. A new Confederacy of southern states was emerging. In February all attention focused on Montgomery, Alabama, where delegates from six freshly seceded states, having just abandoned one Union, met to form another.

"All Montgomery had flocked to Capitol Hill in holiday attire," wrote Thomas Cooper DeLeon, a southern journalist, of the festive day of February 18. "Bells rang and cannon boomed, and the throng—including all members of the government—stood bareheaded as the fair Virginian"—Letitia Tyler, granddaughter of John Tyler—"threw that flag to the breeze. . . . A shout went up from every throat that told they meant to honor and strive for it; if need be, to die for it." In his inaugural address as provisional president, Jefferson Finis Davis, a former U.S. senator from Mississippi who had also served as U.S. secretary of war, spoke of the "wickedness of our aggressors" and stated that if the integrity of southern territory were assailed, the Confederacy must "appeal to arms and invoke the blessings of Providence on a just cause."[8] Georgian Alexander Hamilton Stephens was chosen to be Davis's vice president; the two men's relationship would prove tense as Stephens failed to cooperate with Davis and even pushed for Georgia's secession from the Confederacy.

With the new Confederacy a reality, the likelihood of a military clash between it and the United States increased with each passing day. On March 4, in his inau-

Alabama State Capitol, Montgomery

On February 4, 1861, on the steps of the Alabama capitol, Jefferson Finis Davis took the oath as president of the Confederate States of America.

First White House of the Confederacy, Montgomery, Alabama

Jefferson Davis and his family moved into the first Confederate White House, a simple clapboard structure on the southwest corner of Bibb and Washington (now Lee) Streets. The building was moved in 1921 to a position opposite the state cap:tol.

gural address, Lincoln appealed to the "erring sisters" to maintain peace. But it was too late for words; by early April, the situation had reached the explosive point.

The spark, predictably, came in Charleston. Federal troops had evacuated Fort Moultrie, on Sullivan's Island, on December 26 and moved to Fort Sumter, well out in Charleston Harbor. A supply mission by the steamer *Star of the West* had been turned back by locals on January 9, leaving Major Robert Anderson and his garrison of seventy-six soldiers, eight musicians, and forty-three workmen with limited resources. Former U.S. Army officer P. G. T. Beauregard, now a Confederate brigadier general, supervised the placement of heavy guns bearing on Fort Sumter. Confederates issued an ultimatum that if Anderson did not evacuate the fort, they would commence a bombardment on April 12. Anderson had no plans to move. "I do not pretend to go to sleep," wrote Chesnut. "How can I? If Anderson does not accept terms at four, the orders are he shall be fired upon. I count four, St. Michael's bells chime out, and I begin to hope. At half past four the heavy booming of a cannon. I sprang out of bed, and on my knees prostrate I prayed as I never prayed before."9

Following the fall of Sumter, the Confederate garrison raised their new nation's flag.

National Archives and Records Administration

The bombardment began at 4:30 A.M. when a mortar fired from Fort Johnson, on James Island. Thirty Confederate cannon and seventeen mortars erupted in a pounding barrage. At about 7:30 A.M. the Federals answered from one of their forty-eight heavy guns. The Confederate bombardment went on for thirty-four hours, during which some 4,000 shells were fired into Sumter, setting some buildings ablaze and damaging the fort's brick walls but, remarkably, killing no one. Around noon on April 14, Anderson lowered the colors and evacuated by ship. The action was not completely bloodless: a Union private was killed when a gun exploded as it fired a salute, and another man later died of wounds. The Confederacy had won the war's first engagement. "I've often longed to see a war, and now I have my wish," wrote Louisa May Alcott in distant Concord, Massachusetts.[10]

Now the nation went headlong into war. Three days after Fort Sumter fell, Virginia, the most populous and powerful southern state, seceded. "Well, my dearest one, Virginia has severed her connection with the Northern hive of abolitionists," wrote ex-president John Tyler to his wife, Julia, on April 18, "and takes her stand as a sovereign and independent State. . . . The North seems to be thoroughly united against us. . . . The contest into which we enter is one full of peril, but there is a spirit abroad in Virginia which cannot be crushed until the life of the last man is trampled out."[11]

Another prominent Virginian, Robert E. Lee, now sided with his home state. "With all my devotion to the Union and the feeling of loyalty and duty of an

American citizen, I have not been able to make up my mind to raise my hand against my relatives, my children, my home," he wrote his sister, Anne Marshall, from Arlington on April 20. "I have therefore resigned my commission in the Army, and save in defense of my native State, with the sincere hope that my poor services may never be needed, I hope I may never be called on to draw my sword." On the same day, in his resignation letter to Union general in chief Winfield Scott, Lee repeated this sentiment: "Save in defense of my native State, I never again desire to draw my sword." [12]

The activities of war blossomed across the springtime landscape. On April 18, U.S. troops abandoned the arsenal at Harpers Ferry. The following day the U.S. Navy began a blockade of southern ports. On this day too, riots erupted in Baltimore as troops of the Pennsylvania and Massachusetts militia en route to Washington passed through this city with strong southern sympathies. "A man appeared bearing a Confederate flag at the head of about one hundred rioters," wrote Frederic Emory, and "a savage attack was made against [the Federal soldiers] with stones and other missiles." Emory described the "scene of bloody confusion" that followed: "As the troops retreated, firing, the rioters rushed upon them only to be repulsed by the line of bayonets. Some of the rioters fought like madmen." Arms were taken from the arsenal at St. Louis to prevent their capture by secessionists. "Captain James H. Stokes, of Chicago, late of the regular army, volunteered the undertake the perilous mission," an account in the *Chicago Tribune* on April 29 explained, "and Governor Yates placed in his hands the requisition of the Secretary of War for 10,000 muskets." Stokes had the weapons loaded onto a ship and took them to Alton, Illinois, for transfer to railroad cars. "Rich and poor tugged together with might and main for two hours, when the cargo

Fort Sumter, Charleston Harbor, South Carolina

For all practical purposes, the Civil War began here when well-organized local secessionists under General P. G. T. Beauregard bombarded the fort and drove out its Union garrison.

Artillery Shell, Fort Sumter

This shell embedded in Fort Sumter's brick is likely not from the war-opening bombardment, but from Federal artillery on Morris Island later in the conflict.

The White House, Washington, D.C.

During Abraham Lincoln's years in it, the White House was the site of an almost nonstop series of emergency meetings to plan strategy for the war.

was all deposited in the cars, and the train moved off, amid their enthusiastic cheers, for Springfield."[13]

Neither side was prepared for war, and many in both sections believed the conflict would be brief. "We thought the rebellion would be over before our chance would come," wrote Michael Fitch, a soldier in the 6th Wisconsin Infantry. The gearing up for war—assembling and drilling men, manufacturing and gathering supplies, and shaping the civilian psychology—continued apace. On May 6 Arkansas and Tennessee seceded, and on the twentieth North Carolina cast its lot with the Confederacy. In Washington, no one was quite sure of the direction of the government. "Washington was then a military camp, a city of barracks and hospitals," recalled Noah Brooks, a California reporter. "The first thing that impressed the newly arrived stranger . . . was the martial aspect of the capital. Long lines of army wagons and artillery were continually rumbling through the streets; at all hours of the day and night the air was troubled by the clatter of galloping squads of cavalry; and the clank of sabers, and the measured beat of marching infantry, were ever present to the ear."[14]

The most mysterious inhabitant of the Federal capital seemed to be its leader. "Unquestionably, Western man though he may be, and Kentuckian by birth, President Lincoln is the essential representative of all Yankees," wrote the novel-

The Capitol dome was not yet finished in this 1860 portrait.

National Archives and Records Administration

ist Nathaniel Hawthorne after meeting the commander in chief. "His hair was black, still unmixed with gray, stiff, somewhat bushy, and had apparently been acquainted with neither brush nor comb that morning . . . his complexion is dark and sallow . . . he has thick black eyebrows and an impending brow; his nose is large, and the lines about his mouth are very strongly defined." A description of President Davis, now in Richmond, where the Confederate government had settled, was markedly different. "Was introduced to the President today," wrote John B. Jones, a clerk in the War Office, on May 17. "His stature is tall, nearly six feet; his frame is very slight and seemingly frail, but when he throws back his shoulders he is as straight as an Indian Chief. The features of his face are distinctly marked with character, and no one gazing at his profile would doubt for a moment that he beheld more than an ordinary man." [15]

Across North and South, men were equipping themselves and learning the rudiments of soldiering. Carlton McCarthy, a young volunteer in the Army of Northern Virginia, remembered the first days of his acquaintance with the Richmond Howitzers. "The volunteer of 1861 made extensive preparations for the field," he wrote. "Boots, he thought, were an absolute necessity, and the heavier the soles and longer the tops the better. His pants were stuffed inside the tops of his boots, of course. A double-breasted coat, heavily wadded, with two rows of big brass buttons and a long skirt, was considered comfortable. A small stiff cap, with a narrow brim, took the place of the comfortable 'felt,' or the shining and towering tile worn in civilian life." The monotony of a typical day in drill camp came as an anticlimax for men who had joined the army expecting a great adventure. "When the orderly is satisfied that not one of us has run away and accepted a Colonelcy from the Confederate States since the last roll-call," wrote Theodore Winthrop, a soldier in the 7th New York at Camp Cameron, "he notifies those

U.S. Capitol, Washington, D.C.

On March 4 Lincoln rose on the steps of the Capitol and took the oath as president. During the war, the Capitol became a boardinghouse for soldiers, who camped, drilled, and baked bread in the building's basements and subbasements.

unfortunates who are to be on guard for the next twenty-four hours of the honor and responsibility placed upon their shoulders. Next he tells us what are to be the drills of the day. Then, 'Right face! Dismissed! Break ranks! March!' "[16]

During June 1861 the first land-based actions of the war finally occurred and the youthful soldiers tasted battle—"saw the elephant," as they liked to put it—for the first time. Clearly, for many, it would not be the type of adventure they had envisioned. The actions in Virginia at Philippi (June 3), Big Bethel (June 10), Romney (June 13), and Vienna (June 17) were only skirmishes, but the newspaper accounts were read passionately and on both sides strengthened partisanship.

In Washington and Richmond, the leaders grappled with strategy and tactics. Following the clash at Sumter, Lincoln had called for 75,000 militia to put down the rebellion and asked that they enlist for a period of three months. A major victory during that time would undoubtedly restore the Union, many Yankees felt.

The Virginia Capitol photographed in the spring of 1865.

Library of Congress

Virginia State Capitol, Richmond

Following Virginia's secession, Congress moved the Confederate government to Richmond, closer to the seat of war. The Virginia Capitol served as the Confederate Capitol.

Conversely, southerners believed that a sharp loss for the Yankees in a major battle would close the notion of war. Both sides were dramatically optimistic.

Each side leaned too much toward protecting its capital; each, at this stage, thought in terms of geography rather than destruction of opposing armies. Lincoln clearly relied on the advice of his aging general in chief, Brevet Lieutenant General Winfield Scott, who advocated an "anaconda plan" of controlling the Mississippi River and blockading southern ports, cutting off the Confederates' ability to resupply themselves or trade with other powers.

The North brought to the conflict vastly superior manpower and resources but also faced a far greater task. Fighting an offensive war against the South meant conquering and holding a huge territory with hundreds of miles of coast and inland waters. Moreover, offensive tactical maneuvers almost always result in higher casualties among the attackers than among the defenders, especially defenders with the benefit of interior lines. The North's task was indeed daunting.

Though outweighed in resources and population, the South had a distinct advantage—time was on its side. The longer the war dragged on, the more likely it was that northern civilians would grow weary of fighting simply on arcane constitutional principles. A peace movement might be sparked in the North; meanwhile, intervention from foreign powers such as Britain or France might collapse the Union's ability to wage war.

This was all speculation, however—hope. What each side needed now was commanding officers who could gain success in the field. Major General George B. McClellan's solid victory at Rich Mountain, in western Virginia, on July 11–12 cast him into favorable light with the U.S. War Department. But it was Brigadier General Irvin McDowell, another regular-army mainstay, who would lead the first large Federal army into the field. On July 15 McDowell's 35,000 troops were concentrated around Washington, while another 18,000 Yankees, under Colonel Robert Patterson, were poised between Harpers Ferry and Winchester. Their principal opposition consisted of 20,000 Confederate troops commanded by General P. G. T. Beauregard, the hero of Sumter, and 12,000 commanded by General Joseph E. Johnston.

Beauregard's men were stationed at Manassas, a railroad junction that afforded the opportunity to contest a Union advance toward either Fredericksburg or Culpeper. By July 21 McDowell had maneuvered south via Centreville and

This front view of the Brockenbrough House was made in the spring of 1865.

Library of Congress

John Brockenbrough House, Richmond, Virginia

The new White House of the Confederacy was established at the John Brockenbrough House at 12th and Clay Streets. The stately building served as the official and social hub of Confederate society until the evacuation of Richmond in April 1865.

George N. Barnard photographed the ruins of the Judith Henry House, burned during the battle, in March 1862.

Library of Congress

Henry House Hill, Manassas, Virginia

The first major land action of the war erupted along Bull Run near Manassas, Virginia, on July 21. The climactic fighting took place on Henry House Hill.

was nearing Beauregard's position. The armies would clash along a creek called Bull Run. As the Yankees approached, Johnston arrived to reinforce Beauregard. McDowell's plan was to turn the Confederate left flank by crossing Sudley Springs, on the northernmost part of the field, and cut off the railroad to the Shenandoah Valley. He also sent the division under Brigadier General Daniel Tyler to assault the Stone Bridge crossing Bull Run northeast of Henry House Hill. A detached element of Tyler's would create a diversion at Blackburn's Ford to hold the Confederate troops there in a static position.

Meanwhile, Beauregard was himself planning to attack northward toward Centreville. But on the early morning of July 21 his plans were interrupted. A shell struck near the Wilmer McLean House, where he was breakfasting. The battle had begun.

Beauregard hastily ordered the attack toward Centreville. But confusion reigned and orders were bungled, dissipating the opportunity for striking the Federal left. Beauregard and Johnston reinforced their northernmost line and shifted the bulk of their army toward Henry House Hill. A Federal brigade led by Colonel William T. Sherman forded Bull Run and threatened to flank the Confederate concentration. The southerners withdrew to Henry House Hill. In the early afternoon the brigade of Brigadier General Thomas J. Jackson with-

stood a withering fire and gave renewed hope along the Confederate line. "There is Jackson, standing like a stone wall!" said Brigadier General Barnard Elliott Bee, and the sobriquet of "Stonewall" Jackson was born.[17]

From a distance, it seemed clear that the great battle of the war was under way. The booming of guns could be heard in Washington. In Lynchburg, Susan Blackford wrote, "The sound of the cannon were distinctly heard on the hills of Lynchburg, and we well knew that a great battle was being fought from early morn until sunset, and that not only the fate of our country and homes was at stake, but that each boom which stirred the air might be fraught with the dying sigh of those we loved best."[18]

The Matthews house survived First Bull Run intact, as shown by George N. Barnard's photo made in March 1862.

Library of Congress

Henry P. Matthews House, Manassas

North of Henry House Hill stands the Henry P. Matthews house, known as the Stone House. The structure withstood artillery hits during First Bull Run and served as a hospital following the engagement.

As the afternoon waned, what appeared to be a Confederate panic turned into a great victory. Brigades under Brigadier Generals Edmund Kirby Smith and Jubal A. Early helped turn the battle for Beauregard. The Federal brigades north of Henry House Hill became entangled and confused. Heavy fighting along the Federal right forced McDowell to withdraw in a state of near-chaos, retreating across the Stone Bridge and back toward Washington. "My first impression was that the waggons were returning for fresh supplies of ammunition," wrote the English journalist William Howard Russell. "But every moment the crowd increased; drivers and men cried out with the most vehement gestures, 'Turn back! Turn back! We are whipped.'"

The panic in Washington was even greater. "The dreadful disaster of last Sunday can scarcely be mentioned," wrote the politician Edwin M. Stanton on July 26. "The imbecility of this Administration culminated in that catastrophe—

Stone Bridge, Manassas

Union soldiers surged across the Stone Bridge over Bull Run in attack and then in retreat as the tide of battle turned at First Bull Run.

George Barnard and his colleague James F. Gibson photographed the ruins of the Stone Bridge in March 1862.

National Archives and Records Administration

an irretrievable misfortune and national disgrace never to be forgotten . . . the capture of Washington seems now to be inevitable." Although the Confederates had not gained anything strategically, there was jubilation on their side. "Yesterday we fought a great battle and gained a great victory," wrote Stonewall Jackson to his wife on July 23, "for which all the glory is due to *God alone.*"[19]

The reality of a more protracted war than had been imagined was now becoming clear. The Federal high command lost faith in McDowell and, the day after the gloomy surprise at First Bull Run, placed McClellan in charge of the forces that would become the Army of the Potomac. "By some strange operation of magic I seem to have become the power of the land," wrote McClellan to his wife on July 27. "I almost think that were I to win some small success now I could become Dictator or anything else that might please me."[20]

The main eastern armies, shocked from their first large-scale encounter, settled into a protracted period of relative inactivity. Many soldiers retreated into thinking about the ordinary again: the clothing, the food, the marching, and the bravado. "During the day one of the boys brought in a Virginia paper in which it was stated that one 'Southerner could lick five Northern mudsills,'" wrote Charles E. Davis, a soldier of the 13th Massachusetts, near Hagerstown, Maryland, on August 1. "It was not so very comforting to feel that we were to be killed off in blocks of five." Another Massachusetts soldier, John Billings, later recalled the relative plenty of the early months of the war. "I will now give a complete list of the rations served out to the rank and file, as I remember them," he wrote. "They were salt pork, fresh beef, rarely ham or bacon, hard bread, soft bread, potatoes, an occasional onion, flour, beans, split pease, rice, dried apples, dried peaches, desiccated vegetables, coffee, tea, sugar, molasses, vinegar, candles, soap, pepper, and salt. It is scarcely necessary to state that these were not all served out at one time." Some soldiers had great difficulty adjusting to their agreements with the government, as with the "mutiny" in the 79th New York volunteers at Camp Causten, Maryland, on August 17. "Soon a scene of the wildest confusion took place," wrote William Thompson Lusk, an officer in the regiment. "The soldiers, throwing off all authority, presented the hideous and disgusting spectacle of a debauched and drunken Helotry. It was a time trying to one's nerves—more trying far than the musketry or cannonading of Bull Run."[21]

The next significant action came far to the west, in Missouri. On August 10, Union and Confederate troops clashed along Wilson's Creek near Springfield. The Yankees retreated after losing their fierce commander, Brigadier General Nathaniel Lyon. Confederate Major General Sterling Price occupied Springfield. A month later at Lexington, Confederates attacked a Union brigade and artistically used hay bales as a moving rampart. "Our men looked at the moving monster in astonishment," wrote the English journalist Samuel P. Day. "It lay like a large serpent, winding over the hills and hollows, apparently motionless, yet mov-

Jackson Monument, Manassas

On Henry House Hill, Confederate brigadier general Thomas J. Jackson stood "like a stone wall," earning his famed nickname.

John Ray House, Wilson's Creek, Missouri

Silent witness to the bloody battle of Wilson's Creek on August 10, 1861, the Ray House stands within sight of the infamous Bloody Hill. Following the battle, Brigadier General Nathaniel Lyon, fallen Federal commander, lay in the front parlor.

ing broadside on, to envelop and destroy them in its vast folds. In vain the cannon were turned upon it. The heavy bales absorbed the shot harmlessly."[22]

As the autumn leaves fell and brisk temperatures cooled the landscape, McClellan busied himself with a succession of minor battles against several commanders in western Virginia. At Cheat Mountain on September 11–13, General Robert E. Lee commanded his first battle of the war. Lee had been dispatched to recover ground taken from Brigadier General Robert S. Garnett by McClellan. Cheat Mountain controlled several mountain passes and an important road between Staunton and Parkersburg. Lee's 15,000 men faced 2,000 Yankees commanded by Brigadier General Joseph J. Reynolds. Stalled by poor roads and heavy rains, the Confederates ultimately withdrew on September 15 after an inconclusive fight. This outcome earned Lee the derisive epithet "Granny Lee" for his supposed timidity. McClellan too became a target of criticism. After he sent a telegram proclaiming "all quiet along the Potomac," suggesting a boast that no danger was imminent,[23] the dispatch soon gained a new meaning: McClellan was inactive in pursuing the enemy. So both Lee and McClellan received somewhat harsh treatment in the press during this first autumn of the war.

But it was not all quiet along the Potomac. On October 21 a brief battle flared at Ball's Bluff, near Leesburg, Virginia, between Union troops under Brigadier General C. P. Stone and Confederates commanded by Brigadier General Nathan G. Evans. Stone had been ordered by McClellan to demonstrate against Evans and push him back toward Snicker's Gap. Stone ordered 1,700 men, led by Colonel Edward D. Baker, a politician and close friend of Lincoln's, forward to a point on the Virginia side of the Potomac opposite Harrison's Island. Evans's Confederates, stationed in Leesburg, met the oncoming Yankees and fought a brisk battle that turned into a rout of the northerners. Catching Baker's retreating force against the river, many still crossing it, and without cover, the Rebels inflicted heavy casualties, leaving 49 Union dead (including Baker), 158 wounded, and 714 missing. It was a complete disaster for the Union troops.

Ball's Bluff National Cemetery, Leesburg, Virginia

The smallest National Cemetery holds the remains of one Confederate and fifty-four Union soldiers who died in the battle of Ball's Bluff on October 21, 1861. A Union fiasco, the engagement cost the life of Colonel Edward D. Baker, a close friend of Lincoln's.

"The Virginians and Mississippians being accustomed to the rifle, most of them old hunters, rarely missed their man," wrote Randolph Abbott Shotwell, a soldier in the 8th Virginia Infantry, of the Ball's Bluff fiasco. "Climbing into the tops of trees, creeping through the tall grass, or concealed in the gullies, they plied their weapons with murderous havoc especially among the Federal officers. It was very poor management to allow this to go on." Such tactically mismanaged affairs did not bode well for inexperienced officers trying to win the loyalty of their men. "It does not suit the temper of our fellows to be commanded much," wrote Charles Johnson of the 9th New York Infantry, a unit known as Hawkins's Zouaves, on October 28 near Hampton, Virginia. To illustrate his point, Johnson noted the fate of a Lieutenant Russell of the 9th New York; the unfortunate lieu-

U. S. Grant Birthplace, Point Pleasant, Ohio

Hiram Ulysses Grant entered the world in this rude
house in rural Ohio on April 27, 1822. He would
grow up to change his name to Ulysses S. Grant and
lead his nation's armies in their greatest war.

Nancy G. Eicher

tenant "was burned in effigy, a caricature was made on his tent, and a variety of
greater indignities suggested, should he ever attempt to take command."[24]

Throughout this chaos, inexperienced soldiers led by inexperienced officers
were discovering the realities of war. Out west on November 7, Brigadier General

Ulysses S. Grant, an obscure officer who had resigned from the army before failing in a multitude of civilian jobs before the war, attacked Confederate forces near Belmont, Missouri. Grant's 3,000 troops approached by steamer from Cairo, Illinois, and landed near Belmont opposite the considerable bluffs at Columbus, Kentucky. Grant approached, but did not take, the Confederate stronghold at Columbus, which contained heavy guns and 5,000 troops. The Confederate garrison was commanded by Major General Leonidas Polk. "A strange scene followed," wrote Eugene Lawrence of the initial foray into the Confederate camps. "Grant's troops, carried away by the joy of the moment, having taken several hundred prisoners and the enemy's camp, broke into disorder. Speeches were delivered by excited orators; the captured camp was plundered; in the midst of their enemies the inexperienced soldiers believed themselves secure."[25]

Although Grant's troops withdrew, the attack was held in high esteem by Lincoln, who was growing increasingly frustrated with his inactive commanders. The final important action of the year, Belmont signaled a small spark in U. S. Grant that would grow in significance over the coming months.

A BITTER YEAR OF HARD-FOUGHT WAR

*T*he first cold winter weeks of 1862 brought relative silence to most of the war front, but not to Kentucky. A border state with divided loyalties, Kentucky had seceded in part on November 20, 1861, and was thus counted by both the United States and the Confederacy. The birthplace of both presidents, the state supported nationalism but was strongly tied to the South through its economy. Confederate forces met in November at Russellville to establish an independent government. The commonwealth had a pro-Union legislature and, in Beriah Magoffin, a pro-Confederate governor. Confusion reigned. Neither side recognized the other's government. In effect, Kentucky remained politically neutral. But the struggle for military control of it continued.

Before the commonwealth's partial secession, Confederate brigadier general Felix K. Zollicoffer had occupied the strategic position at Cumberland Gap, the gateway into Kentucky. In November, Zollicoffer had advanced to Mill Springs on the Cumberland River. By January he was joined by Major General George B. Crittenden, the area commander. On January 17 a Federal force under Brigadier General George H. Thomas reached Logan's Cross Roads, about eight miles from Zollicoffer's Confederates. About 4,000 men on each side faced each other in what became known as the battle of Mill Springs. Crittenden ordered an attack and struck Federal cavalry pickets on January 19. Zollicoffer led his brigade into the attack, the men using a ravine for cover as they advanced. Colonel Speed S. Fry, commanding the Federal 4th Kentucky Cavalry, rode forward to reconnoiter and came upon an officer dressed in a white raincoat—it was Zollicoffer. Shots rang out, and Zollicoffer fell dead, hit by three bulllets. Fry, who had fired one of the shots, later became a Union general officer. Thus occurred one of the war's few incidents in which an officer of such high grade killed an opposing general.

Zollicoffer's death caused momentary confusion among the Confederates, but they re-formed and attacked before being pushed back for good. Crittenden withdrew in haste, the Confederate camps were overrun, and many of the southerners deserted in disgust. It was a small but significant victory for the Federal army in Kentucky.

Meanwhile, a larger, strategic campaign for Kentucky was shaping up to the west, where the theater commands were decidedly different on each side. The Federals were commanded by Major General Henry W. Halleck, whose Department of Missouri had 41,000 troops at St. Louis, and Major General Don Carlos Buell, whose Department of the Ohio had 45,000 men arrayed from Louisville to the southern tip of Illinois. The Confederacy, on the other hand, had bestowed its confidence in a single man, General Albert Sidney Johnston, whose 43,000 troops stretched from near Memphis eastward to his base at Bowling Green. Halleck ordered Brigadier General Ulysses S. Grant to move up the Tennessee River as a diversion, masking a move in force by Buell on Nashville. Grant would approach Fort Henry with infantry supported by navy gunboats in one of the war's first combined operations. On February 2–3, Grant began his movement. Halleck forgot to inform Buell, but in the end that made little difference, thanks to Grant's generalship. By February 6, Grant's 20,000 men had moved south to threaten Fort Henry, forcing the Confederate commander, Brigadier General Lloyd Tilghman, to abandon Fort Heiman (opposite Henry on the Tennessee) and withdraw most of Henry's garrison. Tilghman sent most of his men eleven miles east to Fort Donelson, on the Cumberland River.

By 1 P.M. on February 6 the Federal gunboats had forced Fort Henry's remaining defenders to surrender. Grant's success caused an enormous problem for

Zollicoffer Park, Mill Springs, Kentucky
Confederate brigadier general Felix K. Zollicoffer, shot by a Union colonel, died under the tree marked with a red wreath. The tree fell in 1995.

Fort Donelson, Tennessee

During February 1862, little-known Union Brigadier General U. S. Grant led his army against Forts Henry and Donelson, keys to Tennessee. Reconstructed huts in Donelson approximate the officers' quarters as they were during the battle.

Dover Hotel, Dover, Tennessee *(right)*

Following Grant's attack on Fort Donelson, Confederate brigadier general Simon B. Buckner surrendered to Grant at the Dover Hotel.

Johnston, who now had to attack him or allow him to do further damage to the Confederate strategic situation in the area. Johnston reinforced Fort Donelson with 12,000 men under Brigadier General John B. Floyd, formerly James Buchanan's secretary of war. Grant pressed for an advance on Donelson, but poor weather and a lack of naval support on the Cumberland delayed it. James A. Connolly, a Union major, described the trip from Fort Henry to Fort Donelson in a letter written to his wife on March 10: "The ground was strewn with hats, caps, coats, pants, canteens, cartridge boxes, bayonet scabbards, knapsacks, rebel haversacks filled with biscuits of their own making, raw pork, broken guns, broken bayonets, dismounted cannon, pieces of exploded shells, six- and twelve-pound balls, and indeed all sorts of things that are found in the army."[1]

On February 12 Grant's force moved east. The Federal gunboats, under Captain Andrew H. Foote, had little success this time. Fort Donelson's guns, heavier and better placed than Fort Henry's, damaged the ships and forced a withdrawal. Grant's army, now consisting of 25,000, faced 21,000 defenders under Floyd, including troops of Brigadier Generals Simon B. Buckner and Gideon J. Pillow arrayed between Grant and the fort. Early on February 15, the Confederates attempted a breakout. It seemed to be working until Floyd lost his courage and withdrew to the original positions. Heavy fighting continued, with the Federals regaining control of the situation when Floyd escaped with Pillow, both fearing

treason charges if captured. The emerging cavalry legend Lieutenant Colonel Nathan Bedford Forrest also escaped. Early on February 16, Grant received Buckner's communication asking for terms, and replied, "No terms except an unconditional and immediate surrender can be accepted. I propose to move immediately upon your works."[2] Grant thus captured 11,500 men, forty guns, and considerable supplies, becoming one of the North's first bona fide heroes of the war and earning the appreciative nickname "Unconditional Surrender Grant."

As winter slipped away, some heavy action occurred farther west. At the end of 1861, Major General Samuel R. Curtis had taken command of the Army of the Southwest, the principal Union force in Missouri. A Confederate army under Major General Sterling Price was concentrated at Springfield. In February, Curtis hounded Price, who retreated into northern Arkansas to regroup with the troops under Major General Earl Van Dorn and Brigadier General Benjamin McCulloch. Curtis concentrated along Pea Ridge, Arkansas, and awaited a Confederate attack. Van Dorn approached under a driving snowstorm. He deceived the Federals by leaving campfires burning and attacked the Union left near Elkhorn Tav-

Elkhorn Tavern, Pea Ridge, Arkansas

The battle of Pea Ridge, near Springfield, Missouri, enveloped a large area that included Elkhorn Tavern.

ern on March 7, while McCulloch and his force—consisting in part of Indians—sprang forth at Leetown to divert Yankee reserves. McCulloch was killed in the fight. The following day Union troops pushed the Confederates away from Pea Ridge, and Van Dorn abandoned the state. It was a costly strategic loss for the Confederacy.

A room in the Elkhorn Tavern.

"The effects of an army passing over a country distracted by war were now clearly to be seen," wrote William Watson of the 3d Louisiana Infantry about the retreat following Pea Ridge. "Be that army friend or foe, it passes along like a withering scourge, leaving only ruin and desolation behind." Watson also described his fellow soldiers as they straggled in along the retreat. The men "were actually staggering from want and fatigue. Their shoes were worn off their feet, from passing over rocks and boulders, and through creeks. Their clothes were in rags from scrambling through the woods and briars, and burnt in holes from crouching too close to camp fires in their broken slumbers. Their eyes were bleared and bloodshot, from want of sleep and the smoke of the woodfires, and their bodies were emaciated by hunger."[3]

In the East, the winter's quiet would soon give way to a peculiar show of innovative naval technology. The first battle between two ironclads occurred on March 9 at Hampton Roads, Virginia, as the CSS *Virginia* took on the much smaller USS *Monitor.* The *Virginia* was the retrofitted screw steamer *Merrimack,* scuttled by Union forces when they abandoned the Norfolk Navy Yard in April 1861. Confederate naval engineers had turned the hull into a new type of warship with a heavily armored, canted superstructure. The 263-foot-long ship was protected by 4-inch armor laid over 22-inch-thick oak beams. Nothing like it had existed before. The ship's armament consisted of six 9-inch Dahlgren guns and four rifled 6-inch and 7-inch guns. Captain Franklin Buchanan's crew of 350 steamed into Hampton Roads on March 8 to destroy all the Federal ships they could find.

At about 2 P.M. the Virginia rammed the USS *Cumberland* and fired mercilessly on the USS *Congress*. The former sank at 3:30 P.M. and the latter surrendered and was run aground. Then, around 10 P.M., a peculiar vessel arrived, the *Monitor*. The invention of John Ericsson, the ship looked like a flat skiff 172 feet long with a single round turret extending only 9 feet above the waterline; the appearance gave rise to the name "cheese box on a raft." At nine o'clock the next morning, the *Monitor,* commanded by Lieutenant John L. Worden, moved alongside the *Virginia* and opened fire with its two 11-inch Dahlgrens. "The contrast was that of a pygmy to a giant," wrote Gershom J. Van Brunt, commander of the nearby USS *Minnesota*. "Gun after gun was fired by the *Monitor,* which was returned with whole broadsides by the rebels, with no more effect, apparently, than so many pebble-stones thrown by a child."[4] The *Monitor* held off the savage attacks of the *Virginia,* and the Confederate ironclad withdrew from Hampton Roads. It would not play a further role in the war, being scuttled two months later. The *Monitor* itself foundered off Cape Hatteras on December 31, 1862. A new era in naval war had nonetheless emerged.

In the western theater, Grant's success had forced Albert Sidney Johnston southward along a line extending from Memphis through Corinth, Mississippi, to Huntsville, Alabama. Johnston, reinforced by Major Generals Braxton Bragg, who had been in Mobile, and Leonidas Polk, who had been at Columbus, Kentucky, had about 40,000 men under his command. Grant's 35,000 men were encamped by early April south of the Tennessee River at Pittsburg Landing, near Shiloh Church. The area contained a network of creeks and several passable

The Hornets' Nest, Shiloh, Tennessee

The crucial area on April 6 was the Hornets' Nest, where Union troops deployed along a sunken farm road held out against twelve separate Confederate assaults before finally surrendering.

W. Manse George Cabin, Shiloh

In the battle of Shiloh, these peaceful fields surrounding the W. Manse George cabin saw the bloodiest fighting of the war up to that time.

roads. Major General Don Carlos Buell's Army of the Ohio, with its 50,000 men, lay well to the northeast at Columbia. On the night of April 5–6, Johnston, now supported also by P. G. T. Beauregard, advanced northward toward Grant's encampment. Grant did not suspect an attack from the south, but a massive assault came. Johnston hoped to push Grant's army between two creeks, cutting it off from reinforcement via the Tennessee River. Early on the morning of April 6, a battle line stretching from southwest to northeast exploded. "Fill your canteens, boys. Some of you will be in hell before night and you'll need water!" said Isaac C. Pugh, colonel of the 41st Illinois Infantry.[5] The battle of Shiloh, the costliest thus far in the war, had begun.

The magnitude of the battle was evident to soldiers in the ranks from its earli-

Albert Sidney Johnston Tree, Shiloh

Rather than seeking help when he was wounded in the leg at Shiloh, the Confederate commander, Albert Sidney Johnston, bled until he collapsed, fell from his horse, and was carried to the base of this tree as he died.

Bloody Pond, Shiloh

During the vicious combat at Shiloh, wounded soldiers crawled to a watering hole for a desperately needed drink. Their blood gave rise to the pond's macabre name.

est hours. "Suddenly, away off on the right, in direction of Shiloh Church, came a dull, heavy 'Pum,' then another, and still another," wrote Leander Stillwell, a private in the 61st Illinois Infantry. "Every man sprung to his feet as if struck by an electric shock, and we looked inquiringly into one another's faces. . . . Those heavy booms then came thicker and faster, and just a few seconds after we heard that first dull, ominous growl off to the southwest, came a low, sullen, continuous roar. There was no mistaking that sound. That was not a squad of pickets emptying their guns on being relieved from duty; it was the continuous roll of thousands of muskets, and told us that a battle was on."[6]

Johnston left Beauregard in command and rode forward to lead an assault. All along the Union battle line regiments were falling back in the face of the Confederate attack. A division under Brigadier General Benjamin M. Prentiss stubbornly held fast along a sunken farm lane in what became known as the "Hornets' Nest" for the intensity of the fighting there. Twelve separate assaults supported by heavy cannonading had failed to dislodge Prentiss and Brigadier General William H. L. Wallace from the position. As this action flared, Johnston led an attack in which he was wounded behind the knee. The Confederate commander nearly bled to death on his horse and finally slumped off and died near the base of a tree. Command devolved upon Beauregard.

The death of Johnston momentarily stunned parts of the Confederate line, but they pushed forward and successfully pinned Grant's force with its back against the Tennessee River. Meanwhile, Prentiss had finally surrendered the Hornets' Nest, even as wounded soldiers crawled to drink from a small pond nearby. The little body of water became known as "Bloody Pond" after it was stained from the soldiers' wounds. As darkness fell on April 6, the Federal army's position seemed tenuous. Moreover, a rainstorm moved in and depressed the Yankees further.

By daybreak, however, the tide was turning. Although tardy, Brigadier General Lew Wallace had finally arrived to support Grant, and more important, Buell's army had crossed the river to the rescue. Refreshed with three new divisions, Grant attacked on the morning of April 7 and by late morning had forced Beauregard's troops back in disarray. By early afternoon Beauregard had his whole army in retreat southward to Corinth. The Federal movement surprised some soldiers, including the young Confederate and future explorer Henry M. Stanley, who wrote: "I became so absorbed with some blue figures in front of me,

that I did not pay sufficient heed to my companion greys. . . . Seeing my blues in about the same proportion, I assumed that the greys were keeping their position, and never once thought of retreat. . . . I rose from my hollow; but, to my speech-less amazement, I found myself a solitary grey, in a line of blue skirmishers! My companions had retreated! The next I heard was, 'Down with the gun, Secesh, or I'll drill a hole through you! Drop it, quick!'"[7]

Even though Grant and his commanders had been surprised at Shiloh and stood in peril after the first day's fighting, the battle resulted in a strategic blow to the Confederacy as Beauregard retreated south into Mississippi. The cost on both sides had been high, however: some 3,477 men lay dead, and another 20,264 were wounded or missing. The scale of the bloodshed shocked citizens North and South.

At the same time the world saw a grand vision of battle between Johnston and Grant, a Confederate hero was emerging in the Shenandoah Valley. Stonewall Jackson, now a major general, was making trouble for a succession of Union commanders in the fertile region so critical to supplying the war in Virginia. On the Federal side, Major General George B. McClellan had succeeded the aging Winfield Scott as general in chief late in 1861. McClellan ordered Major General Nathaniel P. Banks to harass Jackson and push him out of the Valley. Jackson withdrew from his headquarters in Winchester on March 11 and the two forces clashed at Kernstown on March 23, resulting in a failure for Jackson.

Jackson was a man on a mission, however, charged with a fervent religious doctrine that overshadowed all else. "The religious element seems strongly devel-oped in him," wrote observer Garnet Wolseley, "and though his conversation is

Confederate Burial Trench, Shiloh

Many Union soldiers killed and originally buried on the Shiloh battlefield were later reinterred in the nearby National Cemetery. Confederates were buried in four trenches on the field, one at this marker.

Fort Pulaski, Georgia

Fort Pulaski's forty guns in casements and barbettes commanded the sea approach to Savannah. The fort's loss to the Yankees was a major blow to Georgia and the South.

Following Pulaski's bombardment, Timothy O'Sullivan photographed an interior view of the breach.

Library of Congress

perfectly free from all puritanical cant, it is evident that he is a person who never loses sight of the fact that there is an omnipresent Deity ever presiding over the minutest occurrences in life, as well as over the most important." Jackson indeed took his calling seriously. "You appear much concerned at my attacking on Sunday," he wrote his wife on April 11. "I was greatly concerned, too; but I felt it my duty to do it, in consideration of the ruinous effects that might result from postponing the battle until morning. . . . I hope and pray to our Heavenly Father that I may never again be circumstanced as on that day."[8]

Jackson's brilliance as a tactician, outwitting the Federal forces while keeping them away from other Union armies, came to the forefront during the remainder

Artillery Damage, Fort Pulaski

Fort Pulaski's facade still shows scars from its shelling by the heavy rifled cannon of Union artillerymen. Scattered brick damage remains throughout the fort.

Bonaventure Cemetery, Savannah

As Union army and naval forces approached Savannah from the ocean inlets, a greater cost was taking hold for southern civilians, who were losing their sons in appalling numbers. Many Confederate dead were buried in Bonaventure Cemetery, on the former estate of Confederate navy captain Josiah Tattnall.

Fort Jackson, Georgia

Although Fort Pulaski fell to Federal hands early in the war, nearby Fort Jackson, the oldest brick fort in Georgia, commanded the Savannah River defenses of the city and held out until December 20, 1864, when Sherman's approach forced evacuation of the city.

of his Valley campaign. He thwarted the plans of Banks, Major Generals John C. Frémont and Franz Sigel, and Brigadier General James Shields variously at McDowell (May 8), Front Royal (May 23), Winchester (May 25), Cross Keys (June 8), and Port Republic (June 9).

As the famed Valley campaign was beginning, military events of differing character transpired far to the south. On Cockspur Island, near Savannah, Georgia, Fort Pulaski—one of the great brick-masonry forts of the coastal southeast—fell to Union forces on April 10–11. The fort's thick walls could not withstand the

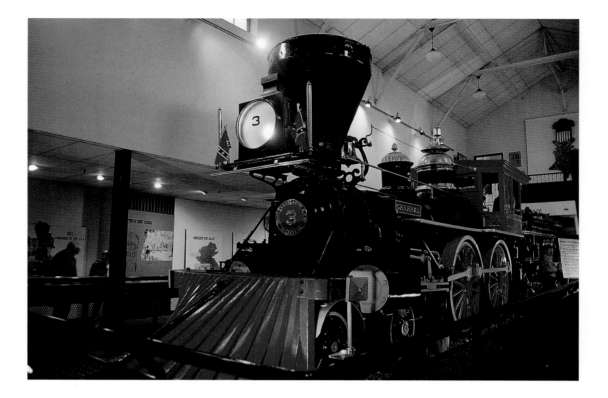

The General, Kennesaw, Georgia

This is the locomotive commandeered at Big Shanty by James J. Andrews and his men in their daring raid in northern Georgia.

fire of batteries of heavy rifled cannon placed one to two miles distant on Tybee Island. The fall of Fort Pulaski, which had been constructed in part under the supervision of a young Robert E. Lee, signaled the demise of brick-masonry forts in the face of the new technology of the rifled cannon.

In northern Georgia at this same time, a band of Yankee spies was about to launch a raid to disrupt the important railroad supply line between Atlanta and Chattanooga. Led by civilian James J. Andrews, the twenty-two volunteers traveled to Big Shanty, where on April 12 they captured a locomotive called the General. The raiders steamed northward, destroying track and telegraph wires along the way, while Confederates chased them with another locomotive, the Texas. Having set a railcar afire to slow the pursuers, Andrews and his men nearly made it to safety in Union-occupied Chattanooga. William Pittenger, one of the raiders, described what happened: "With no car left, no fuel, the last scrap having been thrown into the engine or upon the burning car, and with no obstruction to drop on the track, our situation was indeed desperate. A few minutes only remained until our steed of iron which had so well served us would be powerless."[9] Indeed, the raiders were caught. Andrews and seven others were executed in Atlanta. They and six of the raiders imprisoned for the longest time were the first Americans to receive the Medal of Honor.

If the Confederacy was holding its own in the East that April, the same could not be said for New Orleans. With a population of nearly 170,000, the city was by far the largest in the Confederacy. It was also a vital port for supplying the Mississippi River operations and the Deep South. New Orleans had a garrison under Major General Mansfield Lovell, but its only real defense lay some seventy miles downstream, where Forts Jackson and St. Philip guarded the river. These forts

Tunnel Hill, Georgia

The General's capture became "The Great Locomotive Chase" when the engine was pursued by the Texas. On their way north the engines passed through Tunnel Hill, south of Ringgold. The trackless wartime tunnel (right) can still be seen next to a post-war tunnel now used for freight trains.

Graves of the Andrews Raiders, Chattanooga National Cemetery

Eight of the Andrews raiding party were executed as spies. Their bodies were sent to Union-held Chattanooga and now are buried in the Chattanooga National Cemetery.

and their 500 men, along with several ships, attempted to block a Federal fleet commanded by Captain David G. Farragut, who had twenty-four wooden vessels and nineteen mortar boats. After bombardment failed to subdue the forts, Farragut managed to slip past them by night; he then sailed upriver and captured New Orleans without firing a shot. The citizens were now under Federal occupation. "These people have complimented us highly," wrote New Orleanian Julia LeGrand on April 25. "To quell a small 'rebellion,' they have made preparations enough to conquer a world." A well-known northerner viewed the problem from a slightly different perspective. "We woo the South 'as the Lion wooes his bride,'" wrote Nathaniel Hawthorne, in Concord, Massachusetts, the following summer. "It is a rough courtship, but perhaps love and a quiet household may come a bit at last." [10]

If the loss of New Orleans was a terrible blow to the South, the military action involved was almost microscopic in comparison with the great eastern campaign about to unfold on Virginia's Peninsula. Lincoln and most of his advisers favored a movement by land against Richmond, as had been attempted the previous summer. McClellan, however, hatched a plan to transport his troops by ship to the eastern tip of the Peninsula and approach Richmond from the southeast. After considerable argument and consternation, McClellan got his way.

On April 2, McClellan arrived at Fort Monroe, the point of embarkation, where 50,000 Federal troops were massed for the Peninsular campaign. Confederate Major General John B. Magruder represented the first line of defense, with 13,000 troops. The main Confederate army between McClellan and Richmond was that of General Joseph E. Johnston, which consisted of about 43,000 men, most of them at Yorktown. McClellan was bluffed by Magruder's movements and therefore laid siege to Yorktown rather than attacking it. For a month he was inactive, preparing for a heavy bombardment of the Confederate defenses. But on May 3 Johnston withdrew toward Richmond and the Federal army struck at his rear guard, opening the battle of Williamsburg. Despite his army's lackluster performance in this engagement, McClellan celebrated the battle in a letter to his wife written on May 6. "As soon as I came upon the field the men cheered like fiends," he wrote, "and I saw at once that I could save the day. I immediately reinforced Hancock and arranged to support Hooker, advanced the whole line across the woods, filled up the gaps, and got everything in hand for whatever might occur. The result was that the enemy saw that he was gone if he remained in his position, and scampered during the night." [11]

Johnston's force of 60,000 now moved close in to defend Richmond, north and east of the city. McClellan's army, now numbering 105,000, established a base at the White House on the Pamunkey and threatened the James River with gunboats that moved as far north as Drewry's Bluff, a mere seven miles from Richmond. As panic struck the capital, with the booming of cannon plainly heard, life for the 38,000 citizens soured. "Oh, the extortioners!" wrote John B. Jones, a clerk in the War Office, on May 23. "Meats of all kinds are selling at fifty cents per

Beaver Dam Creek, Virginia

The second battle of the so-called Seven Days, on June 26, 1862, took place near Mechanicsville, along Beaver Dam Creek.

pound; butter, seventy-five cents; coffee, a dollar and half; tea, ten dollars; boots, thirty dollars per pair; shoes, eighteen dollars; ladies' shoes, fifteen dollars; shirts, six dollars each." [12] On May 31 the armies clashed along the Richmond and York River Railroad at Fair Oaks Station in the battle of Seven Pines. A muddy confrontation complicated by poor weather, the engagement presented an opportunity for Confederate success, but the chance slipped away. Moreover, the Confederate commander, Johnston, was wounded and carried from the field. But this

Sarah Watt House, Gaines's Mill, Virginia
(Overleaf)

During the third of the Seven Days, at Gaines's Mill, the Watt House served as Yankee brigadier general Fitz John Porter's headquarters.

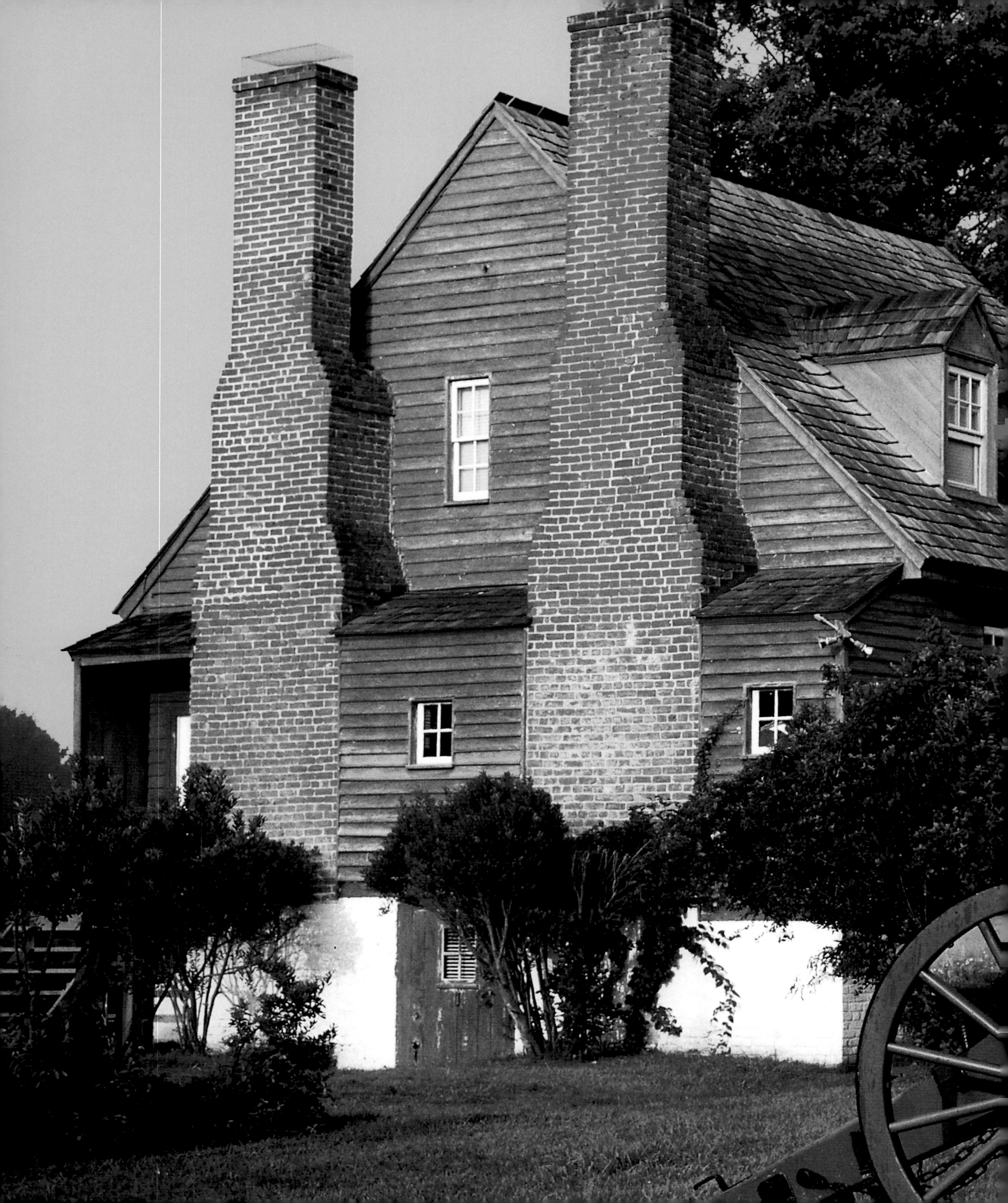

latter event, seemingly ill-omened, would prove to be providential for the Army of Northern Virginia.

The replacement for Johnston was General Robert E. Lee, who had been assisting President Davis in Richmond. In the army, soldiers had little indication of the great association to come. "General Lee had up to this time accomplished nothing to warrant the belief in his future greatness as a commander," wrote Colonel Evander M. Law. "The general tone, however, was one of confidence, which was invariably strengthened by a sight of the man himself. Calm, dignified, and commanding in his bearing, a countenance strikingly benevolent and self-possessed, a clear, honest eye that could look friend or enemy in the face, clean-shaven, except a closely-trimmed mustache which gave a touch of firmness to the well-shaped mouth; simply and neatly dressed in his uniform of rank, felt hat, and top boots reaching to his knee; sitting his horse as if his home was in the saddle." [13]

The casualties at Seven Pines were high: 5,031 Yankees and 6,134 Confederates. When bleeding and broken troops were carried into Richmond, the result was stunning. "The people realized with a sudden shock the actualities of an internecine strife and it was brought to their very doors," wrote Alexander Hunter, a soldier in the 17th Virginia Infantry. "Before, they had seen only its pride and pomp, and a martial showing; they had heard only the rattling of artillery over stony streets, and the tread of passing columns; but all at once, with the sound of hostile guns, gaunt, grim-visaged war touched their hearts, and sickened their souls with horror." [14]

McClellan moved most of his force south of the Chickahominy River and, characteristically, waited. The weather was poor, and several weeks passed with no significant action. Then, on June 25, the armies began a series of battles that collectively came to be called the Seven Days. On June 25 occurred the battle of Oak Grove. A larger action, the battle of Mechanicsville, was fought along Beaver Dam Creek the following day. Lee's sound plan went awry when Stonewall Jackson arrived late for his attack and Brigadier General A. P. Hill attacked without orders. The following day Lee and his subordinates attempted to regroup. Robert Stiles, a young soldier in the Richmond Howitzers, described seeing a brief encounter between Lee and Jackson. "The two generals greeted each other warmly, but wasted no time upon the greeting," he wrote. "They stood facing each other, some thirty feet from where I lay, Lee's left side and back toward me, Jackson's right and front. Jackson began talking in a jerky, impetuous way, meanwhile drawing a diagram on the ground with the toe of his right boot. He traced two sides of a triangle with promptness and decision; then starting at the end of the second line began to draw a third projected toward the first. This third line he traced slowly and with hesitation, alternately looking up at Lee's face and down at his diagram, meanwhile talking earnestly; and when at last the third line crossed the first and the triangle was complete, he raised his foot and stamped it down with emphasis, saying 'We've got him.'" [15]

White Oak Swamp, Virginia

The sixth of the Seven Days battles occurred on June 30. McClellan pulled back behind the White Oak Swamp, an almost impassable marsh. Stonewall Jackson pursued and launched an uncoordinated artillery barrage.

The White Oak Swamp photographed between 1861 and 1865.

Library of Congress

The bloody battle fought on June 27 was called Gaines's Mill. Lee planned to envelop Brigadier General Fitz John Porter's right, but again Jackson was slow. A massed Confederate assault late in the afternoon turned the battle into a southern victory. "Going on to the field, I picked up a tent and slung it across my shoulder," wrote Oliver W. Norton, a soldier in the 83d Pennsylvania Infantry, of Gaines's Mill. "The folds of that stopped a ball that would have passed through me. I picked it out, put it in my pocket, and, after firing sixty rounds of my own and a number of wounded comrade's cartridges, I came off the field unhurt, and ready, but not anxious, for another fight." On June 28, as McClellan began a retreat to the James River, the lesser battle of Garnett's and Golding's Farms took place. The following day the armies clashed at Savage's Station. Jackson struck the Federal army from the north at the White Oak Swamp on June 30. And finally, on July 1, Lee's army attempted to crush the retreating Federals with a frontal attack at Malvern Hill, but his men were hammered by well-placed Union artillery. Confederate guns fired with great effect as well. As Thomas L. Livermore, a New Hampshire soldier, described it, "Shells flew all around us, and the wonder was that more were not hurt. I turned my head to the left and saw the battery and the gunners, springing to their work amid the smoke. I saw one pull the string, saw the flash of the piece, heard the roar, and the whiz of the shell, heard it burst, heard the humming of the fragments, and wondered if I was to be hit, and quicker than a flash something stung my leg on the calf, and I limped out of the ranks, a wounded man."[16]

McClellan's Peninsula campaign was a strategic failure. On July 3 he withdrew the Army of the Potomac to Harrison's Landing to await transportation north. On July 12 Lee dispatched Jackson north to Gordonsville to threaten the advance of Major General John Pope, whose Army of Virginia occupied the Shenandoah Valley. Thus began the Second Bull Run campaign. Jackson hit Banks at Cedar Mountain on August 9 in an affair that was significantly mismanaged on both sides. Subsequently, both armies moved north, and in late August, Jackson launched a movement around Pope's army, interposing himself between Pope and Washington. "His sun-burned cap was lifted from his brow, and he was gazing toward the west, where the splendid August sun was about to kiss the distant crest of the Blue Ridge, which stretched far away, bathed in azure and gold," wrote Jackson's staff officer Robert L. Dabney of his celebrated commander. "And his blue eye, beaming with martial pride, returned the rays of the evening with almost equal brightness. . . . his face beaming with delight, [he] said, 'Who could not conquer, with such troops as these?' "

The opposing Federal commander did not enjoy such praise from his fellow soldiers. Pope's competence had been brought into question a number of times, and a common feeling of distrust had developed among many toward him. As Union brigadier general Samuel D. Sturgis put it on August 23, "I don't care for John Pope one pinch of owl dung." [17]

The armies converged on the old battleground of Bull Run, which had seen

Malvern Hill, Virginia

The final affair of the Seven Days took place at Malvern Hill on July 1. Lee attempted to hit the withdrawing Federals hard with a coordinated attack but failed. Nearly 250 Federal cannon protected the hill.

such carnage the previous summer. Pope's 75,000 men faced the 55,000 commanded by Lee. By August 27 Jackson had concentrated his forces at Manassas Junction, capturing a vast array of Union supply trains. Major General James Longstreet approached from the west. By dawn on August 29, Federal troops occupied the old battleground at Henry House Hill and the towns of Centreville and Haymarket, and lay scattered southward toward Brentsville. Pope planned to attack Jackson from both east and west, but as Second Bull Run began, the Federal attacks westward were poorly coordinated, piecemeal affairs. Vicious fighting erupted at Groveton and along an unfinished railroad cut passing along the base of Jackson's position at Stony Ridge. To many soldiers, the scenes of combat were unforgettable. "I can see him now," wrote Edward McCrady of Confederate brigadier general Maxcy Gregg, "as with his drawn sword, that old Revolutionary scimitar we all knew so well, he walked up and down the line, and hear him as he appealed to us to stand by him and die there. 'Let us die here, my men, let us die here.' And I do not think that I exaggerate when I say that our little band responded to his appeal, and were ready to die, at bay, there if necessary."[18]

Groveton Monument, Manassas, Virginia

The Groveton Monument, erected in 1865, honors the Union dead of Second Bull Run, which ended in Confederate victory.

On August 30, the battle's second day, a massive attack by Longstreet on the southern end of the Union line produced a great Confederate victory. Jackson was enabled to strike at Pope's northern flank, and the Federal army fell back to the old battlefield on Henry House Hill. Pope withdrew toward Centreville, but a rear-guard action ensued on September 1 at Chantilly, where the Confederate divisions of Major Generals Dick Ewell (who had lost his leg at Groveton on August 28) and A. P. Hill struck Federal forces commanded by Major General Philip Kearny and Brigadier General Isaac I. Stevens. The Confederates were turned back, but both Kearny and Stevens were killed. Charles F. Walcott, a captain in

Kearny and Stevens Monuments, Chantilly, Virginia

The Second Bull Run campaign concluded with a rear-guard action at Chantilly, where two beloved Union generals were killed. Major General Philip Kearny inadvertently rode into the Confederate lines; Brigadier General Isaac I. Stevens was hit in the head by a Minié bullet. Their small monuments are all that remains of the battlefield, now engulfed by suburban development.

the 21st Massachusetts Infantry, described Kearny's death. "The General, entirely alone," he wrote, "apparently in uncontrollable rage at our disregard of his peremptory orders to advance, forced his horse through the deep, sticky mud of the cornfield past the left of the regiment, passing within a few feet of where I was standing. I watched him moving in the murky twilight through the corn, and, when less than twenty yards away, saw his horse suddenly rear and turn, and half-a-dozen muskets flash around him: so died the intrepid soldier, Gen. Philip Kearny!"[19]

Only days after the close of the Second Bull Run campaign, another major campaign commenced. Pope had lost any remaining credibility, and his army was absorbed into McClellan's Army of the Potomac. Lee, on the other hand, was gaining confidence hourly and planned to bring the fight onto northern soil for the first time, easing war-torn Virginia, foraging in Maryland, perhaps winning support from Marylanders with southern sympathies, and maybe—with a victory fairly won on northern ground—gaining recognition from Britain or France. He crossed the Potomac on September 4 and three days later was in Frederick, aiming to strike north toward Harrisburg, Pennsylvania, and cut the major east-west railroads relied on by the Federals. The hoped-for revolution by Marylanders did not materialize, but the southerners met little military resistance at first. McClellan pursued only slowly, with vast overestimations of Lee's strength in mind. On September 13 he was given a copy of Lee's Special Order No. 191—a copy meant for Rebel major general D. H. Hill had been dropped. The order contained Lee's complete plan for his northern campaign. Here was an amazing piece of luck. Just as amazingly, McClellan did nothing for more than sixteen hours. By the time he did move, Lee had learned of the lost order.

The first clashes occurred at South Mountain on September 14 as Hill attempted to block Turner's Gap. The Federal 9th Army Corps commander, Major General Jesse L. Reno, was killed there. To the south, at Crampton's Gap, Major General William B. Franklin attacked Confederates under Major General Lafayette McLaws. Meanwhile, Lee had dispatched Jackson to capture the strategically located town of Harpers Ferry, which Jackson accomplished in splendid style on September 15. He then moved to rejoin Lee's main body, which lay to the north at the town of Sharpsburg.

The battle of Antietam, fought in the fields of a north-south line running through Sharpsburg and chiefly to its north and east, would be the bloodiest single-day of the war. On September 17, as Lee's 52,000 men and McClellan's 75,000 soldiers grappled in a series of encounters along Antietam Creek, some 4,808 men would be killed, with another 21,326 wounded or missing. It began as Major General Joseph Hooker's 1st Army Corps struck southward early in the morning, toward Jackson's Corps. Hooker, who was himself wounded in the action, surged through the North Woods and into the cornfield of David R. Miller's farm, one of the scenes of heaviest carnage. "Every stalk of corn in the northern and greater part of the field was cut as closely as could have been done with a knife," Hooker wrote, "and the slain lay in rows precisely as they had stood in their ranks a few moments before. It was never my fortune to witness a more bloody, dismal battlefield."[20]

The fighting throughout the morning spread southward to the West Woods, where Jackson was stubbornly defending an area surrounding the Dunkard Church, a little white landmark near the center of the field. Lee directed the battle from a headquarters in Sharpsburg. McClellan watched from afar at the Philip

Jesse L. Reno Monument, Fox's Gap, South Mountain, Maryland

South of Turner's Gap, at Fox's Gap, heavy fighting erupted on September 14. The Reno Monument marks the spot where the Federal major general was mortally wounded; he died nearby under an oak tree.

The Mountain House, Turner's Gap, South Mountain, Maryland

The Mountain House at Turner's Gap on South Mountain witnessed the first action in Lee's Maryland campaign.

Dunkard Church, Sharpsburg, Maryland

One focus of the early action in the bloody battle of Antietam was the Dunkard Church, a small whitewashed structure operated by a sect of German Baptist Brethren. A storm demolished the church in 1921; it was rebuilt with mostly original materials in 1962.

Samuel Mumma Cemetery and Farmhouse, Sharpsburg

Located in the Antietam battlefield's center, the Samuel Mumma farmhouse (background) and cemetery witnessed heavy action. The house burned during the battle; only the springhouse is original. The cemetery contains the plots of about 165 local citizens, including the Mummas.

Pry house to the northeast. Intense fighting raged around the Samuel Mumma farmhouse and its accompanying cemetery—the house was set ablaze by retreating Confederates. Waves of Union attacks pushed southward toward a sunken farm road that would acquire the name Bloody Lane before the day was out. Colonel John B. Gordon, helping to direct the Confederate regiments huddled in Bloody Lane, was wounded five times this day. "I fell forward and lay unconscious with my face in my cap," recalled Gordon, "and it would seem that I might have been smothered by the blood running into my cap from this last wound but for the act of some Yankee, who, as if to save my life, had at a previous hour during the battle, shot a hole through the cap, which let the blood out."[21]

The fearsome nature of the battle rocked even hardened combat soldiers. "The mental strain was so great that I saw at that moment the singular effect mentioned, I think, in the life of Goethe on a similar occasion—the whole landscape for an instant turned slightly red," wrote David Thompson of the 9th New York Infantry. Another Federal soldier, Frank Holsinger, tried to shrug off the danger: "How natural it is for a man to suppose that if a gun is discharged, he or some one is sure to be hit. He soon finds, however, that the only damage done, in ninety-nine cases out of a hundred, the only thing killed is the powder! . . . I have frequently heard the remark that it took a man's weight in lead to kill him."

In the midst of the chaos, young Rob Lee, the commanding general's son, found himself briefly at his father's headquarters. "General Lee was dismounted, with some of his staff around him, a courier holding his horse," the younger Lee wrote. "Captain Poague, commanding our battery, the Rockbridge Artillery, saluted, reported our condition and asked for instructions. The General, listening patiently, looked at us—his eyes passing over me without any sign of recogni-

The grisly task of burying the dead commenced within hours of the Confederate retreat, as with these Confederates photographed by Alexander Gardner at Bloody Lane on September 19.

Library of Congress

Sunken Road, Sharpsburg

A little farm lane etched into the landscape provided a natural rifle pit for Confederate defenders. Waves of Yankee attacks eventually captured the position, but not before it had fully earned the name Bloody Lane.

tion—and then ordered Captain Poague to take the most serviceable horses and men. . . . As Poague turned to go, I went up to speak to my father. When he found out who I was he congratulated me on being well and unhurt. I then said: 'General, you are going to send us in again?' 'Yes, my son,' he replied with a smile. 'You must all do what you can to help drive these people back.'"[22]

As the afternoon aged, the battle flared farther to the south, where Union

Henry Piper Farmhouse, Sharpsburg

The Piper house stood in the thick of the action at Antietam and was used briefly for a council of war by Confederate generals James Longstreet, D. H. Hill, and Richard H. Anderson. The structure is now the only inn where one can spend a night on the middle of a major Civil War battlefield.

Joseph Sherrick Farmhouse, Sharpsburg

While moving to assault the Confederate at Antietam, Ambrose Burnside's 9th Corps came under fire from batteries on a ridge above the Joseph Sherrick farm (background).

Lower Bridge, Sharpsburg

The Lower Bridge over Antietam Creek was later called Burnside Bridge for the Union general who crossed it rather than fording the shallow creek out of range of sniper fire. Many Federal soldiers were picked off crossing the narrow bridge.

major general Ambrose E. Burnside was supposed to bring his 9th Army Corps across Antietam Creek and strike the Confederates from the east. Burnside delayed for hours and then finally crossed the Lower Bridge (later called Burnside Bridge) in a thin column that led to the slaughter of many of his troops. Burnside's movement and pressure from the area of Bloody Lane pushed the Confederates back toward Sharpsburg, but the "Light Division" of A. P. Hill arrived from Harpers Ferry in time to mount a thunderous counterattack that ended the day's action. Neither side could claim decisive victory. McClellan had not destroyed Lee's army, and Lee had failed in his strategic goals, retreating south of the Potomac on September 19.

There was one important strategic goal accomplished for the Lincoln administration, however. The "victory" at Antietam (measurable at least by Lee's retreat) allowed the president to issue a preliminary proclamation to emancipate slaves in areas in rebellion against the United States. It would be the first move in transforming the war into something more complex than merely a struggle to preserve the Union. Lincoln's preliminary proclamation, issued on September 22, concluded, "On the first day of January in the year of our Lord, one thousand eight hundred and sixty-three, all persons held as slaves within any state, or designated part of a state, the people whereof shall then be in rebellion against the United States shall be then, thenceforward, and forever free."[23]

For the moment, the proclamation seemed to change nothing in the field, particularly for the Union soldiers, many of whom struggled with changing their philosophical goals from the preservation of the Union to freeing the slaves. In

Burnside Bridge photographed by Alexander Gardner in September 1862.

Library of Congress

The Private Soldier, Antietam National Cemetery, Sharpsburg

The Private Soldier, *nicknamed "Old Simon," watches over Antietam National Cemetery, which holds the graves of about 4,695 soldiers.*

both armies, more practical concerns such as clothing, ammunition, and food dominated the everyday thinking. "What in Heaven's name it was composed of, none of us ever discovered," wrote Abner Small of his rations in the Army of the Potomac. "It was called simply 'desiccated vegetables.' . . . I doubt our men have ever forgotten how a cook would break off a piece as large as a boot top, put it in a kettle of water, and stir it with the handle of a hospital broom. When the stuff was fully dissolved, the water would remind one of a dirty brook with all the dead leaves floating around promiscuously. Still, it was a substitute for food. We ate it, and we liked it, too."[24]

In the western theater, Major General Earl Van Dorn led his 22,000 Confederates against Major General William S. Rosecrans's 23,000 at Corinth, Mississippi. The armies clashed on October 3–4, and the Federals succeeded in driving Van Dorn south before he escaped to Holly Springs. "My company was fearfully cut up in this last charge," wrote Oscar Jackson, a captain in the 63d Ohio Infantry. "I saw the fire was aimed at me and tried to avoid it but fate willed otherwise and I fell right backwards, indeed 'with my back to the field and my feet to the foe.' I was struck in the face. I felt as if I had been hit with a piece of timber, so terrible was the concussion and a stunning pain went through my head. I thought I was killed. It was my impression that I would never rise, but I was not alarmed or distressed by the thought that I was dying; it seemed a matter of indifference to me."[25]

Four days after the action at Corinth, General Braxton Bragg's 22,500 Confederates, along with Major General Edmund Kirby Smith's force of 10,000, struck Major General Don Carlos Buell's 60,000 at Perryville, Kentucky. The brutal

Oak Home, Corinth, Mississippi

Used as a headquarters by Confederate general Leonidas Polk before Shiloh, the Oak Home in Corinth, Mississippi, stands in superb condition today.

James S. Jackson Marker, Perryville, Kentucky

Serene fields around Perryville, Kentucky, erupted in action on October 8, 1862, when Buell's Yankees met Bragg's Confederates. The marker stands where Federal brigadier general James S. Jackson was killed in action.

John Morrow House, Prairie Grove, Arkansas

The John Morrow House, now relocated from its original position, served as Confederate major general Thomas Hindman's headquarters before the battle of Prairie Grove. The action, which ended with a Confederate retreat, was the last of any significance in northwestern Arkansas.

fight lasted all day on October 8, with attacks and counterattacks producing casualties but little tactical advantage. In the end Bragg retreated from the field, leaving his dead and wounded behind, and Buell, who had the opportunity for a decisive victory, failed to gain it. Action in the western theater continued intermittently into the winter. At Prairie Grove, Arkansas, a battle erupted on December 7 when 11,000 Confederates under Major General Thomas C. Hindman attacked Federal forces commanded by Major Generals James G. Blunt and Francis J. Herron. The result was inconclusive, although Hindman retreated. Afterward, Federal officers found men without wounds who had simply frozen to death on the ground.

As winter deepened, one more great battle in the East would mark the year's end. "Fellow-citizens, we cannot escape history. . . . We shall nobly save or meanly lose the last, best hope of earth," Lincoln had told Congress on December 1.[26] By all odds, the strategy adopted by the new commander of the Army of the Potomac, Major General Ambrose E. Burnside, would meanly lose. Lincoln, fed up with inactivity and excuses, had shelved McClellan following Antietam. The president found in Burnside a leader lacking confidence but tried him anyway.

Chatham, Fredericksburg, Virginia

The J. Horace Lacy estate, Chatham, saw the Yankees advance around Falmouth, across the Rappahannock River from Fredericksburg, and into the fortified heights of the town.

Unfortunately for the Federals, Burnside had an ill-conceived plan. He moved south to Falmouth, Virginia, across the Rappahannock River from Fredericksburg. His strategy called for Major Generals Edwin V. Sumner and Joseph Hooker to cross pontoon bridges and fight their way through the city (which had 5,000 residents), even though the attack would be uphill toward well-fortified artillery positions. Meanwhile, Major General William B. Franklin would attack Jackson to the south along the Richmond, Fredericksburg, and Potomac Railroad. With victory in Fredericksburg, the ultimate prize of Richmond would be within grasp.

Burnside originally hoped to catch Lee's army divided as it had been in late November, with Longstreet in the Wilderness and Jackson in the Valley. But the

USS *Cairo*, Vicksburg, Mississippi

On December 9, 1862, during Grant's first campaign to take Vicksburg, the USS Cairo, a Federal ironclad river gunboat, struck two torpedoes (naval mines) and sank on the Yazoo River. Raised in the 1960s, the rebuilt remains of the ship stand adjacent to a museum of associated artifacts.

Innis House, Fredericksburg

The heaviest fighting at Fredericksburg came at Marye's Heights, where Union troops were slaughtered. The Innis House still contains many clapboards pockmarked by small-arms fire.

Salem Church

West of Fredericksburg stands Salem Church, where civilians huddled during the battle. During the Chancellorsville campaign, on May 3, 1863, a hot fight ensued around the church, and brick damage remains visible today. After the engagement the church served as a hospital, the blood on the floorboards so abundant it accumulated in puddles.

bridge engineering met delays, and by December 13, the day of the battle, the Confederate forces were reunited. Lee deployed Longstreet along Marye's Heights, a northwest-southeast ridge running along the rear of the town, and Jackson to the south at Prospect Hill and Hamilton's Crossing.

Fredericksburg was essentially two battles. The "slaughter" of Fredericksburg took place at Marye's Heights, where onrushing Yankees met their deaths against a stone wall and sunken road used by Confederate defenders. Watching the struggle from a position now called Lee's Hill, General Lee commented, "It is well that war is so terrible, or we should grow too fond of it." The battle against Jackson was more of a contest, with Brigadier General George G. Meade penetrating the Confederate line briefly before a counterattack by Jackson and inaction on Franklin's part stalled the engagement. By day's end, the fearful casualties—particularly on the Union side—and frigid weather horrified the participants. "At last, outwearied and depressed with the desolate scene," wrote Joshua L. Chamberlain, lieutenant colonel of the 20th Maine Infantry, "my own strength sunk, and I moved two dead men a little and lay down between them, making a pillow of the breast of a third. There was some comfort even in this companionship."[27]

The desperate loss at Fredericksburg seemed to intensify a feeling of dread in the North as 1862 came to a close. Only one class, buoyed by Lincoln's Emancipation Proclamation, felt a wave of optimism. "It will make justice, liberty, and humanity permanently possible in this country," Frederick Douglass told a British audience in November. "We are all liberated by this proclamation," he later said. "It is a mighty event for the bondman, but it is a still mightier event for the nation at large."[28]

ZENITH OF THE CONFEDERACY

$\mathcal{A}$s the desperate year 1863 began, the great hope of the Confederacy expanded into its full glory. The nation was now clearly in a long-term war, a vicious struggle in which the sectional differences would break apart the country into principalities. In all theaters, the military situation seemed to favor the Confederacy. The South had the momentum and the spirit. Lee's Army of Northern Virginia had been turned back from northern soil the previous autumn, but it had scored a stunning victory at Fredericksburg just two weeks be-

Chicago Board of Trade Battery, Stones River, Tennessee

After his retreat from Perryville, General Braxton Bragg concentrated at Murfreesboro, Tennessee. Near this town his force collided with Yankees under Rosecrans on December 31, 1862, and January 2, 1863, in the battle of Stones River. The Chicago Board of Trade Battery's six guns checked a Confederate assault during the action.

William B. Hazen Brigade Monument, Stones River, Tennessee

The first Civil War monument stands along the railroad line near Murfreesboro on the Stones River battlefield. Erected in 1863 by soldiers of Colonel William B. Hazen's brigade, the stone cube commemorates the stand made by Hazen's troops in this thick area of battle, dubbed "Hell's Half Acre." The graves of fifty-six fallen members of Hazen's brigade surround the monument.

fore New Year's Day. Braxton Bragg's inconclusive campaign in Tennessee had nevertheless turned away the Federal army under William Rosecrans—enough so that Bragg could telegraph President Davis from the battlefield at Stones River that God "granted us a victory." In the West, John C. Pemberton seemed to be holding off a repeated succession of attacks aimed at capturing Vicksburg, the Confederate stronghold on the Mississippi. The sun was shining brightly on Confederate fortunes.

The Confederacy's military necessities were still far different from those of the Union. Rebel armies were fighting essentially a defensive war, hoping that the North's citizens would grow weary of it and that Britain or France would recognize the southern nation. As long as the Federals had to attack southward, sustaining heavy losses, and as long as the daring of commanders such as Lee and Jackson paid off, the Confederacy could look forward to increasing odds for a peace movement and an armistice. The chances looked good in the first few weeks of 1863, and during the coming months they would look even better.

For the armies in the field, the new year began quietly; winter's cold precluded campaigning. As the Confederacy anticipated a spring thaw and a new series of victories, the aims of the war were slowly changing in Washington. The Emancipation Proclamation, which had taken legal effect on New Year's Day, would transform the struggle into a holy war for freedom in the minds of many northerners. It would no longer be simply a fight to restore the Union, but for a nobler, higher cause. In the first days and weeks of the year, however, that idea had not yet taken hold; Lincoln's proclamation was new, and few people, northern or southern, grasped its enormous significance.

As for the men in the ranks, whatever their thoughts about emancipation, they already knew that their adventure was titanic and the scale of the destruction appalling. The horrors of Antietam and Fredericksburg were still fresh in the memories of soldiers in the East. "In every direction around men were digging graves and burying the dead," wrote David Hunter Strother, a western Virginian colonel in the Federal army, following Antietam. Strother's prose and art in *Harper's Weekly* carried the lighthearted pseudonym "Porte Crayon," but there was nothing light in his description of the carnage he had seen. Many of the dead, he wrote, "were black as Negroes, heads and faces hideously swelled, covered with dust until they looked like clods. Killed during the charge and flight, their attitudes were wild and frightful. One hung upon a fence killed as he was climbing it. One lay with hands wildly clasped as if in prayer. From among these loathsome earth-soiled vestiges of humanity, the soldiers were still picking out some that had life left and carrying them in on stretchers to our surgeons."[1]

The new year brought Abraham Lincoln face-to-face with an old problem: where to find an adequate commander for the Army of the Potomac. Lincoln had removed Ambrose Burnside from command after the disaster at Fredericksburg but had no ideal replacement in mind. In desperation he turned to Major General Joseph Hooker, a brash, forty-eight-year-old, hard-drinking egotist. Lincoln wrote Hooker, "I have heard, in such a way as to believe it, of your recently saying that both the Army and the Government needed a Dictator. Of course it was not for this, but in spite of it, that I have given you the command. Only those generals who gain successes, can set up dictators. What I now ask of you is military success, and I will risk the dictatorship. . . . And now, beware of rashness. Beware of rashness, but with energy and sleepless vigilance go forward and give us victories."[2] The great eastern Union army had a new chief.

In the South, confidence in Lee and Jackson was soaring. Confederate captain John Esten Cooke, a thirty-two-year-old staff officer of Major General Jeb Stuart's, reflected on Stonewall. "No general was ever so beloved by the good and pious of the land," he wrote. "Old ladies received him wherever he went with a species of enthusiasm, and I think he preferred their society and that of clergymen to any other."[3]

Although the great spring campaigns were still far away, the opening weeks of 1863 did not go totally without important fighting. On January 10–11, Yankees under Major General John A. McClernand and Acting Rear Admiral David Dixon Porter attacked the Confederate stronghold Fort Hindman at Arkansas Post, Arkansas, on the Arkansas River. Some 32,000 men, together with three ironclads and six gunboats, assaulted the fort, garrisoned by three brigades commanded by Brigadier General Thomas J. Churchill and Colonel John W. Dunnington. The action demonstrated the value of river gunboats in shelling a position, as Porter's murderous bombardment contributed substantially to the surrender of the fort and more than 5,000 Confederates—a major loss to the South.

In the East, little of note occurred until March 17, when a cavalry battle erupted at Kelly's Ford, Virginia. Three weeks earlier, Confederate brigadier general Fitzhugh Lee's cavalry had stunned a series of Federal outposts, taking 150 prisoners. Lee left a note for a Federal brigadier general, his old friend William Woods Averell, asking Averell to "return the favor and bring some coffee." Averell arrived at Kelly's Ford on the Rappahannock before sunrise, and the battle was joined at about noon. Both mounted and dismounted, the troopers fought all afternoon, the Yankees repulsing Lee's attacks with a fieldpiece. Major John Pelham, a youthful artillerist and favorite among Lee's command, was killed. The battle ended inconclusively except that Union cavalry had withstood their legendary opponents with great skill. Averell indeed left behind coffee for his old friend.

While such scattered, moderate-sized engagements were taking place, the possibilities for a large, pitched battle between the eastern armies were growing. At the end of April the armies approached each other west of Fredericksburg along the Rappahannock and the Rapidan. "Fighting Joe" Hooker marched the Army of the Potomac—the "finest army on the planet," he called it—westward from Falmouth, hoping to hit Robert E. Lee quickly and hard. But Lee had no intention of being taken off guard; he positioned his Army of Northern Virginia near a crossroads called Chancellorsville.

Hooker's battle plan was solid. One-third of the enormous Union army would

Catherine Furnace, Chancellorsville, Virginia

During Stonewall Jackson's impressive flank march around the Union right at Chancellorsville, his men passed the stone stack of this iron-manufacturing operation, now in ruins, at Catherine Furnace on their way to surprising and scattering the Yankees.

assault Lee's flank and rear; another third, under Major General John Sedgwick, would repeat Burnside's maneuver of attacking across the river at Fredericksburg and plowing westward. The final third of the Federal army would lie in reserve. On April 29, Federal troops crossed the Rappahannock.

At first the situation looked poor for the southerners, who were in danger of being crushed by the pincer movement. Lee's army of 60,000, much undersupplied, faced Hooker's 75,000 and Sedgwick's slowly advancing 40,000. Rather than a Confederate disaster, however, Chancellorsville would be Lee's masterpiece. The bold commander gambled by splitting his army and relying on Stonewall Jackson for a crucial role. Jackson's corps smashed into the Union army on May 1, unleashing a tremendous firefight. That evening Lee and Jackson held a war council, and the following day Jackson led his corps on a fourteen-mile flank march around the Federal right. Late in the afternoon Jackson's men struck the Union right, crushing Hooker's lines. "The events of the few hours of this afternoon and evening are imprinted on my memory in a grand picture," wrote Captain Thomas L. Livermore of the 18th New Hampshire Infantry. "I can now, and probably always shall be able to again bring before my eyes the dusty plain bounded by long lines of men on all sides; the smoke of musketry and batteries, whose thunders still reverberate in my ears."[4]

For the Army of Northern Virginia, jubilation and confidence were the order of the day. Johann August Heinrich Heros von Borcke, an officer on Jeb Stuart's staff, proclaimed: "A more magnificent spectacle can hardly be imagined than that which greeted me when I reached the crest of the plateau, and beheld on this side the long lines of our swiftly advancing troops stretching as far as the eye could reach, their red flags fluttering in the breeze, and their arms glittering in the morning sun; and farther on, dense and huddled masses of the Federals flying in utter rout toward the United States Ford."[5]

But the emerging victory came at a great cost to the Confederacy. While riding into a patch of woods alongside the Orange Turnpike, Stonewall Jackson was fired on accidentally by his own men. Jackson's chaplain, James Power Smith, described the effects of the shooting: "Under this volley, when not two rods from the troops, the general received three balls at the same instant. One penetrated the palm of his right hand and was cut out that night from the back of his hand. A second passed around the wrist of the left arm and out through the left hand. A third ball passed through the left arm half-way from shoulder to elbow. The large bone of the upper arm was splintered to the elbow-joint, and the wound bled freely."[6] Jackson was carried off the field, his left arm was amputated, and plans were made to transport him by ambulance to a railroad station and on to Richmond.

While Lee directed the battle and worried over Jackson, Hooker was having a disastrous day. Not only had he ignored the admonitions of his corps commanders regarding Confederate troop movements, persuading himself that Jackson's corps was retreating, but the next day he was wounded and temporarily dazed.

Stonewall Jackson Mortal Wounding Monument, Chancellorsville, Virginia

This shaft marks the spot where the great Confederate general fell mortally wounded by his own men.

Ellwood Cemetery, Wilderness, Virginia

After Stonewall Jackson's left arm was amputated at an aid station just west of the Chancellorsville fight, friends of the dying commander buried the arm in the family cemetery at the J. Horace Lacy house, Ell-wood.

Chandler Farm Office, Guinea's Station, Virginia

In a small room in the farm office building of the Thomas C. Chandler farm, Fairfield, Stonewall Jackson died of pneumonia on May 10, 1863.

Leaning on a column at the Chancellorsville Tavern, which he employed as a headquarters, Hooker was knocked to the ground when a shell hit the column. "General Hooker was lying down I think in a soldier's tent by himself," wrote Major General Darius N. Couch of the period following the incident. "Raising himself a little as I entered, he said: 'Couch, I turn the command of the army over to you.' . . . This was three-quarters of an hour after his hurt. He seemed rather dull, but possessed of his mental faculties."[7]

The Confederate victory was complete. Although Sedgwick had battled his way westward from Fredericksburg and a sharp fight erupted about Salem Church, Hooker's force was demoralized. Hooker was discredited completely, the Union army on the retreat. Lee could celebrate a terrific victory, save for his concern about Jackson. Eight days after his wounding, Stonewall Jackson died at Guinea's Station, Virginia, his last words reputedly being "No, no, let us cross over the river, and rest under the shade of the trees." The South had lost its most celebrated general of the hour. Much later a former Federal general, Oliver O. Howard, wrote: "Stonewall Jackson was victorious. Even his enemies praise him; but, providentially for us, it was the last battle that he waged against the American Union. For, in bold planning, in energy of execution, which he had the power to diffuse, in indefatigable activity and moral ascendancy, Jackson stood head and shoulders above his confrères, and after his death General Lee could not replace him."[8]

If the news from Virginia cheered southerners, Confederate military prospects in the western theater soon appeared less benign. Along the Mississippi River, the Rebel bastion at Vicksburg was the target of Federal operations moving north from New Orleans and south from Tennessee. The first campaign for Vicksburg had originated in the autumn of 1862 when Ulysses S. Grant struck south along the railroads following the battle of Corinth. He accomplished little except to discover that maintaining long and imperiled supply lines over this route was too problematic.

Old Burial Ground, Grand Gulf, Mississippi

Soon after recrossing the Mississippi River on his way to Vicksburg, Grant fought and won battles at Port Gibson and Grand Gulf. Little remains of the Grand Gulf battlefield, but one sight for the visitor is the Grand Gulf Burial Ground, a decrepit and mostly antebellum cemetery.

In April 1863 the stubborn Federal general opened a second campaign to control the Mississippi. This time Grant marched his troops south through Louisiana until they were below Vicksburg, crossed the Mississippi, and prepared to attack eastward. It was one of the most daring military maneuvers attempted to that time, and required long and tenuous lines of supply and communication. As the campaign began, Union brigadier general Benjamin H. Grierson led a diversionary raid from La Grange, Tennessee, to Baton Rouge, confusing the Confederate response to the impending assaults. "Much of the country through which we passed was almost entirely destitute of forage and provisions," wrote Grierson. "It was but seldom that we obtained over one meal per day. Many of the inhabitants must undoubtedly suffer for want of the necessities of life, which have reached most fabulous prices."[9]

Confederate forces consisted of the garrison at Vicksburg, under Lieutenant General John C. Pemberton—a northern-born officer who nonetheless enjoyed the good graces of Jefferson Davis—and an army near Jackson commanded by Joseph E. Johnston. During the first two and a half weeks in May, Grant's men accomplished an amazing feat: they marched eastward following a battle at Port Gibson and fought and won four battles, separating the two Confederate forces, casting off Johnston into a northward retreat, capturing Jackson, and turning to

Governor's Mansion, Jackson, Mississippi

When Grant's forces captured Jackson on May 14, 1863, Sherman seized the Mississippi Governor's Mansion. Here Grant, Sherman, and Major General James B. McPherson conferred on strategy.

attack Vicksburg from the east. It was a stunning entrance into what became a siege of Vicksburg itself.

The fierce determination of the Federal campaign was reflected in a letter Major General William Tecumseh Sherman wrote toward the end of the siege. "Vicksburg contains many of my old pupils and friends," wrote Sherman, who for a time before the war had been a college superintendent in Louisiana. "Should it fall into our hands I will treat them with kindness, but they have sowed the wind and must reap the whirlwind."[10]

In the city itself, Pemberton and his strong defensive lines held off the Yankee juggernaut, but life for the soldiers and the civilians alike was slowly becoming unbearable. Food was scarce and matériel was dwindling rapidly, and although the Rebel army had repeatedly fought off attacks, its ability to do so was diminishing. The psychological effect on the southerners was exhausting. In March a northern civilian who found himself trapped in the besieged city wrote a diary entry: "The slow shelling of Vicksburg goes on all the time, and we have grown indifferent. It does not at present interrupt or interfere with daily avocations, but I suspect they are only getting the range of different points; and when they have them all complete, showers of shot will rain on us all at once."[11] Many soldiers on both sides and the townsfolk lived in cellars, caverns, or earthen caves carved out of the landscape, approximating crude bombproofs. The same diarist later penned, "The cellar is so damp and musty the bedding has to be carried out and laid in the sun every day, with the forecast that it may be demolished at any moment. The confinement is dreadful. To sit and listen as if waiting for death in a horrible manner would drive me insane."

The suffering continued through May and June as the siege dragged on with infrequent heavy attacks but scattered, intense, nearly continuous skirmishing

Abandoned Graveyard, Champion Hill, Mississippi

The Confederate commander at Vicksburg, Lieutenant General John C. Pemberton, sent forces eastward to attack Grant's rear. The ensuing battle at Champion Hill on May 16 saw attacks and counterattacks before the Yankees retained possession. Few antebellum artifacts remain on the hill apart from this deserted and overgrown cemetery.

Willis-Cowan House, Vicksburg, Mississippi

As Grant's army slowly strangled Vicksburg, Pemberton, the Confederate commander, established headquarters in the Willis-Cowan House.

James Shirley House, Vicksburg

A single important wartime structure survives on the Vicksburg battlefield, the James Shirley House. A prominent battlefield landmark, it was often referred to by soldiers as the White House. Members of Colonel Jasper A. Maltby's 45th Illinois Infantry constructed numerous bombproofs in the ground surrounding the house.

Wisconsin Monument, Vicksburg

Grant's siege, initiated in May 1863, dragged on for more than two months. Confederates defended a ring of forts including Fort Hill, the Stockade Redan, the 3d Louisiana Redan, and the Great Redoubt. Yankees like those depicted on the Wisconsin Monument attempted furious attacks on these positions.

along the lines north, east, and south of the city. One of the most notable attempts to break the lines occurred only three days after the siege began. Engineers working under the supervision of Captain Andrew Hickenlooper, chief engineer of the 17th Army Corps, had constructed a mine under the 3d Louisiana Infantry Redan, the principal fort protecting the Old Jackson Road approach into town, and filled the tunnel with 2,200 pounds of black powder. On May 25 Hickenlooper touched off the explosives as a prelude to a massive attack.

Later, Hickenlooper recalled the scene: "At the appointed moment it appeared as though the whole fort and connecting outworks commenced an upward movement, gradually breaking into fragments and growing less bulky in appearance, until it looked like an immense fountain of finely pulverized earth, mingled with flashes of fire and clouds of smoke, through which could occasionally be caught a glimpse of some dark objects—men, gun-carriages, shelters, etc."[12]

The explosion was spectacular, but the attack failed; so did a similar attempt six days later. The siege at Vicksburg ground on. At this point few Yankees were certain of the competency of Grant, and few Confederates impressed by the abilities of Pemberton. Meanwhile, events in the eastern theater were heating up and drawing attention back to Virginia and Maryland, where the most powerful Rebel and Yankee armies were beginning to maneuver northward.

Robert Edward Lee now had the supreme confidence of his men and of the southern nation, and he believed his Army of Northern Virginia could do nearly anything he asked. He needed much from them, no doubt, as the Confederacy was feeling the crunch of a war that had lasted two years, killing many of its young men, exhausting many of its resources, and destroying much of Lee's beloved Virginia. As the summer of 1863 approached, Lee sought a plan for an offensive that would strike fear into the northern populace, accelerate northern cries for peace, carry the burdens of the war away from Virginia, and perhaps gain foreign recognition for the Richmond government. That might loose enough resources to halt the Yankee appetite for war and prove the salvation of the Confederacy. It was a bold gamble, but such risks had worked in a tactical sense before. Now Lee needed a grand strategic victory, and Pennsylvania would be the target.

The time seemed ripe. The Army of the Potomac was in disarray. Haunted by the failures at Fredericksburg and Chancellorsville, the soldiers utterly lacked confidence in Joe Hooker. Lincoln had no choice but to change commanding generals once again, this time opting for the bookish and occasionally quick-tempered major general George Gordon Meade—reputedly after the senior corps commander, Major General John F. Reynolds, declined the assignment.

On June 9, as the armies began moving northward, a great cavalry battle erupted at Brandy Station, near Culpeper, Virginia. It would be the largest cavalry battle ever fought in North America, and the Yankees under Brigadier General Alfred Pleasonton held their own against the fabled Jeb Stuart's horsemen. As the Confederates moved toward Pennsylvania, screened by the Blue Ridge Mountains, Hooker and then Meade groggily pursued. Stuart squandered the opportunity to keep Lee well informed, instead riding circuitously around the Federal army.

The entire Confederate movement was really a giant raid. Lee had no intention of attempting to occupy Pennsylvania. But he could strike toward Harrisburg, York, or even Philadelphia, terrorizing the North's secure citizenry and

16th Ohio Artillery Monument, Vicksburg

Pemberton's predicament grew with each day. The well-supplied Union artillery blasted away at the Rebel works, grinding down the Confederate ability to go on. Among the batteries employed was the 16th Ohio Artillery, commanded by Captain James A. Mitchell and memorialized by this stone monument.

Illinois Monument, Vicksburg

Grandest of the Vicksburg monuments is the Illinois Monument, which contains the names of all soldiers from Illinois who participated in the Vicksburg campaign.

perhaps winning a pitched battle on Yankee soil. By the last days and hours of June, the Confederate corps under Lieutenant General A. P. Hill, particularly the division under Major General Henry Heth, was moving slowly eastward toward Gettysburg.

Also in the vicinity of Gettysburg, a major convergence of roads, was a brigade of Federal cavalry under Brigadier General John Buford. When the two forces clashed first early in the morning of July 1, neither side anticipated a battle at that position or at that time. But piecemeal attacks and counterattacks escalated as Confederate reinforcements moved in from the west and, eventually, under Lieutenant General Richard S. Ewell, from the north. Buford's cavalry stubbornly resisted the Confederate infantry for a short time before Reynolds's 1st Corps arrived and deployed west of town. Shortly thereafter, Reynolds was killed. "He had taken his troops into a heavy growth of timber on the slope of a hill-side, and, under their regimental and brigade commanders, the men did their work well promptly," wrote Joseph Rosengarten, a major in the Union army. "Returning to join the expected divisions, he was struck by a Minié ball, fired by a sharpshooter hidden in the branches of a tree almost overhead, and killed at once; his horse bore him to the little clump of trees, where a cairn of stones and a rude mark on the bark, now almost overgrown, still tells the fatal spot."[13]

Pushed back through the town by superior Confederate forces, the Federals made a stand on Cemetery Hill, where Major General Winfield Scott Hancock, dispatched by Meade to command the field, assembled the men in order. By the end of the first day, Union corps were still marching toward the field. Meade himself had not yet arrived. Yet Hancock had analyzed the situation with foresight and formed the basis for a fishhook-shaped battle line that would hold the

Unfinished Railroad Cut, Gettysburg, Pennsylvania

Some of the first fighting at Gettysburg raged at a railroad cut, unfinished at the time, before the Confederates pushed the outnumbered northern troops into a general retreat toward the town.

John F. Reynolds Death Monument, Gettysburg

This monument stands at the spot in McPherson's Woods where Union general John F. Reynolds was killed on the first day at Gettysburg.

Pennsylvania Monument, Gettysburg

Gettysburg became the largest battle ever fought in the Western Hemisphere. The stately Pennsylvania Monument commemorates the contributions made by some 30,000 Pennsylvania troops.

high ground east and south of the town—Culp's Hill, Cemetery Ridge, and the Round Tops, neighboring hills on the southern terminus of the Federal formation. Lee, desperately attempting to control a fight that had spiraled away too quickly, deployed Ewell to the north, assigning him the task of taking Cemetery Hill, while A. P. Hill and Lee's most experienced corps commander, Lieutenant General James Longstreet, formed along a ridge running south from the town's Lutheran Theological Seminary.

1st Maryland Eastern Shore (U.S.) Infantry Monument, Gettysburg

The second day at Gettysburg, July 2, 1863, proved one of the most fearsome of the war. Some of the heaviest fighting occurred on Culp's Hill, where Colonel James Wallace's 1st Maryland Eastern Shore volunteers helped stave off Confederate advances.

Beginning early in the morning of July 2, major portions of the battle lines exploded, and intense fighting at various points flared all through the day, many attacks and counterattacks capturing and recapturing the same parcels of ground. The fight for Culp's Hill required several bloody Confederate attacks, the position having been captured by the Federals after dark. Cemetery Hill, with the town's small plot, Evergreen Cemetery, erupted into a scene of terror (a sign beside the small cemetery gatehouse warned that anyone using firearms on the premises would be prosecuted). Huge attacks moved on such spare words as those of Hancock, who at one point snapped: "Do you see those colors? Take them!" Regions of the battleground were soon littered with dead men and horses from both sides: the Wheatfield, Devil's Den, the Peach Orchard, the Rose Farm, the Trostle Farm, and Little Round Top. Federal major general Daniel E. Sickles foolishly marched his 3d Corps past the Trostle Farm into the Peach Orchard, exposing it to heavy fire from Longstreet's huge corps. Sickles's salient might have caused a disaster for the Union; as it was, the 3d Corps fell back and Sickles lost his right leg after it was struck by a cannonball.

It was now clear that a great battle was under way, and many soldiers felt that

1st New York Artillery Monument,
Wheatfield, Gettysburg

*On July 2 one of the most vicious areas of fighting
centered on the Wheatfield, where repeated attacks
and counterattacks could not decisively capture the
ground, now marked in part by the 1st New York
Artillery Monument.*

Little Round Top, Gettysburg

*After scrambling up Little Round Top on July 2,
Union engineers saw that it afforded an ideal position
for artillery overlooking their own lines.*

8th Pennsylvania Cavalry Monument, Gettysburg
(Overleaf)

*The 8th Pennsylvania Cavalry, one of many units en-
gaged in cavalry actions on the bloody second day at
Gettysburg, is memorialized on Hancock Avenue.*

the war would turn on the outcome. It soon also became clear—at least to Major General Gouverneur K. Warren, Meade's chief engineer—that Little Round Top was the key position. Artillery posted on this craggy, rocky hill could command the field. (Big Round Top, a.k.a. Round Top, was too heavily wooded to serve usefully.) A scramble ensued and elements of the Union 5th Corps posted themselves along the ridge of Little Round Top.

The Confederates wanted Little Round Top too. The attack came from Major General John Bell Hood's division of Longstreet's Corps. Hood's soldiers faced a long assault over a relatively open stretch, a slight elevation to the boulder field of the Devil's Den, and then an uphill march through the draw between Round Top and Little Round Top. During the maneuver Hood himself was wounded and lost the use of his left arm. "With this wound terminated my participation in this great battle," he later wrote. "As I was borne off on a litter to the rear, I could but experience deep distress of mind and heart at the thought of the inevitable fate of my brave fellow-soldiers . . . and I shall ever believe that had I been permitted to turn Round Top mountain, we would not only have gained their position, but have been able to finally rout the enemy." [14]

The Confederate attack was indeed aimed at turning the Federal army's left flank, running behind its line, and collapsing it northward, a movement that might have won the battle. The small regiment posted on the extreme left of Little Round Top on the warm afternoon was the 20th Maine Infantry, commanded by Colonel Joshua L. Chamberlain, a former professor at Bowdoin College. As the repeated attacks struck along the lines from the woods, Chamberlain's 20th Maine was running desperately low on ammunition. It was a moment of crisis for the Union cause at Gettysburg. "A critical moment has arrived, and we can remain as we are no longer," wrote Theodore Gerrish, a private in the

Gouverneur K. Warren Monument, Little Round Top, Gettysburg

The summit of Little Round Top affords a panoramic view of the Gettysburg battlefield. The bronze statue depicts Union Major General Gouverneur K. Warren, Meade's chief engineer, who saw the crucial value of holding this hill.

20th Maine. "We must advance or retreat. It must not be the latter, but how can it be the former? Colonel Chamberlain understands how it can be done. The order is given 'Fix bayonets!' and the steel shanks of the bayonets rattle upon the rifle barrels. 'Charge bayonets, charge!'" [15]

Although Gerrish's account is embellished (he was not present at the battle and no such order was dispatched), the passage helped to promote the legendary fight of the 20th Maine on Little Round Top, which did send Colonel William Oates's Alabamians downhill in a scramble. Other actions along the crest of Little Round Top helped hold the position for the Federal army, and the many other concurrent fights slowly wound down into the silent campfires of the night.

The second day at Gettysburg may have decided the battle, but the next day, July 3, would offer its greatest spectacle. Dissatisfied with the prospect of pulling away without a decisive victory, Lee ordered a desperate charge toward the one area that had not been struck forcefully the previous day—the Union center, held by none other than Hancock's 2d Corps. In hindsight it was a foolish move, and

Photographer Alexander Gardner moved the body of a Confederate soldier some forty yards into position among these rocks to heighten this photograph's dramatic appeal. The image was made on July 6, 1863.

Library of Congress

"Confederate Sharpshooter's Position," Devil's Den, Gettysburg

Devil's Den, a field of granite outcrops west of Little Round Top, afforded cover for the brisk rifle battle that rang through the surrounding valley, which in turn earned the name "Valley of Death" for the carnage there.

some commanders—most notably Longstreet—chafed at the idea on the spot. But Lee reasoned that if he could split the Union center, he could drive a wedge through the army and rout the Yankees yet; he also believed the Federal guns were running low on ammunition.

The frontal attack was set for the afternoon of July 3. Divisions under Major General George E. Pickett and Brigadier Generals James J. Pettigrew and Isaac

R. Trimble would mount it. Altogether, more than 12,000 men would march more than a mile across the plain toward a copse of trees and an angle in the stone wall, beyond which Union blue, bristling with rifles and ordnance, blanketed the landscape.

A relative silence at noontime didn't last long. "The cannonade in the center soon began, and presented one of the most magnificent battle-scenes witnessed during the war," wrote Evander M. Law, the Confederate brigadier general who inherited Hood's division. "Looking up the valley toward Gettysburg, the hills on either side were capped with crowns of flame and smoke, as 300 guns, about equally divided between the two ridges, vomited their iron hail upon each other." [16]

96th Pennsylvania Infantry Monument, Gettysburg

Northwest of Little Round Top the 96th Pennsylvania Infantry, commanded by Lieutenant Colonel William H. Lessig, held this position from the late afternoon of July 2 through the battle's end.

The artillery barrage, designed to soften up the Union center for the assault, carried on in full force as the assembled southerners prepared to move out of the woods. In Longstreet's words, "Pickett said, 'General, shall I advance?' The effort to speak the order failed, and I could only indicate it by an affirmative bow." [17] Pickett scurried to the assembled troops, blaring, "Up, men, and to your posts! Don't forget today that you are from old Virginia."

The attack proceeded, the Union soldiers momentarily stunned at the vision of such a huge line of gray moving toward them. The Federal artillery belched long-range shell, shot, and finally short-range canister, and waves of bluecoats poured sheets of fire into the approaching Rebels. It was a desperate moment of the war. As Edmund Rice, lieutenant colonel of the 19th Massachusetts Infantry, recalled, "Voices were lost in the uproar; so I turned partly toward them, raised my sword to attract their attention, and motioned to advance. They surged forward, and just then, as I was stepping backward with my face toward the men, urging them on, I felt a sharp blow as a shot struck me, then another; I whirled round, my sword torn from my hand by a bullet or shell splinter. My visor saved my face, but the shock stunned me." Rice won the Medal of Honor for his action that afternoon. Another Federal officer, Colonel Frank Haskell, remembered the chaos: "The line springs—the crest of the solid ground with a great roar, heaves forward

High Water Mark Monument, Gettysburg

The High Water Mark Monument, located at the point of deepest penetration of the Union center during Pickett's climactic charge on July 3, symbolizes the peak of the Confederate military effort.

**20th Maine Infantry Monument,
Little Round Top, Gettysburg**

On the afternoon of July 2 the 20th Maine Infantry made its now-legendary stand here, holding the extreme Union left against repeated Rebel attacks.

its maddened load, men, arms, smoke, fire, a fighting mass. It rolls to the wall—flash meets flash, the wall is crossed—a moment ensues of thrusts, yells, blows, shots, and indistinguishable conflict, followed by a shout universal that makes the welkin ring again, and the last and bloodiest fight of the great battle of Gettysburg is ended and won." [18]

Gettysburg indeed had ended. The spectacular attack was a failure. Most of those who had marched toward the Union line were dead, wounded, or captured. The

**Grant-Pemberton Surrender Interview
Monument, Vicksburg**

On July 3 Pemberton met Grant at this position, feeling that surrender on July 4 would gain the most favorable terms he could hope for from the Federal commander. On July 4 Grant's troops moved into the city—Independence Day was not celebrated in Vicksburg for the next eighty-six years.

following day Lee withdrew southward, back toward Virginia. Meade's battered force was too depleted of energy, ammunition, and supplies, to pursue with any meaning. The psychological blow to the Confederate war effort would be a major one, although many of the soldiers did not see it that way at the time. To make matters worse, on the same day Lee withdrew, the siege at Vicksburg ended as Pemberton and his remaining Confederates surrendered to Grant. The double victory marked a major turning point of the war, the "high water mark" of the Confederate armies, and the beginning of the end for the Confederate nation.

At Vicksburg, the celebration of the weary Union troops was vigorous, the

Vicksburg National Cemetery, Vicksburg

Grant's success came with a heavy price. The Federal casualties during the campaign amounted to 1,514 dead and 7,848 wounded or missing. Altogether, some 17,000 Union men lie buried in Vicksburg National Cemetery, a forty-acre burying ground established in 1866.

Soldier's Rest Confederate Cemetery, Vicksburg

Confederate losses were great at Vicksburg, but the exact numbers are not clear. Some 1,600 Confederates are buried in Soldier's Rest Cemetery, a plot within Vicksburg's City Cemetery. Three important officers lie within this ground—John S. Bowen, Martin E. Green, and Isham W. Garrott.

terms offered by Grant typically magnanimous. "As soon as our troops took possession of the city, guards were established along the whole line of parapet, from the river above to the river below," wrote Grant. "The prisoners were allowed to occupy their old camps behind the intrenchments. No restraint was put upon them, except by their own commanders." [19]

In Washington, although he was disturbed over Meade's lethargic pursuit of Lee, Lincoln finally had something big to celebrate with the fall of Vicksburg.

Rosalie Mansion, Natchez, Mississippi

Down the Mississippi in Natchez, the fall of Vicksburg signaled the end of a way of life. Union officers raised black troops in Natchez and employed one of the city's elegant mansions, Rosalie, as a headquarters.

"The Father of Waters again goes unvexed to the sea," he wrote a friend.[20] Equally important, he had found at Vicksburg the commanding general he needed.

As the news was unfolding at Gettysburg and Vicksburg, significant events also marked the summer of 1863 along the Atlantic coast and at a gateway into the Deep South.

In Charleston, South Carolina, the hotbed of rebellion, the Federal navy and army made slow progress by a series of movements on land and water. A naval attack in April by Rear Admiral Samuel F. Du Pont failed, but in July the Federal army initiated another set of engagements, designed to disable the forts protecting Charleston Harbor. The troops would assault James Island and Morris Island, capture Fort Wagner and Battery Gregg, and place guns to concentrate fire on Fort Sumter.

Leading the attack on Fort Wagner across a thin strip of sand was Colonel Robert Gould Shaw's 54th Massachusetts Infantry, a national regiment of black American soldiers, one of the first deployed in combat. The attack became a test of whether black American troops could fight effectively. An account of the attack of July 18 published in the *New York Tribune* records the outcome: "In the midst of this terrible shower of shot and shell they pushed their way, reached the Fort, portions of the Fifty-fourth Massachusetts, the Sixth Connecticut, and the Forty-eighth New York dashed through the ditches, gained the parapet, and engaged in a hand-to-hand fight with the enemy, and for nearly half an hour held their ground, and did not fall back until nearly every commissioned officer was shot down."[21] The attack failed, but the gallant efforts of Shaw's regiment

James Island, South Carolina

The war in South Carolina came alive in the summer of 1863. On July 16 Federal troops, including the celebrated 54th Massachusetts Infantry, clashed with Confederates on James Island, a prelude to an all-out attack on nearby Morris Island.

Morris Island, South Carolina

The attack on Fort Wagner on Morris Island came on July 18, across a narrow strip of beach. The 54th Massachusetts led the attack—portrayed in the movie Glory—which failed. The site of Fort Wagner is now under water; this area of beach lies close by.

strongly supported the emerging role of black Americans in the crucial first summer of emancipation.

As the hot and deadly summer moved toward autumn, the western armies positioned for a great clash in the vicinity of Chattanooga. The importance of the railroads at the Tennessee city and the geographical nature of the region made Chattanooga vitally important. The city served as the portal to the Deep South. In June the Army of the Cumberland, under Major General William S. Rosecrans, moved south against General Braxton Bragg's Army of Tennessee. The same armies had grappled in the bloody but strategically inconclusive slugfest at Stones River at the outset of the year. Now Rosecrans sought to push Bragg south and capture Chattanooga. Bragg fortified the city and entrenched but was forced in September to move south after Rosecrans's army crossed the Tennessee River.

Cumberland Gap, Tennessee

Cumberland Gap, Tennessee, served as a natural gateway for the war in Kentucky. Critical in 1863 because its possession controlled the Chattanooga rail line heading east, the gap was recaptured September 8–10 by Union soldiers under Ambrose Burnside.

Bragg massed his forces at Lafayette, Georgia, and engaged some of them with small, isolated Federal elements. He then marched his force to a position along Chickamauga Creek, a little riverway named in Cherokee dialect for a smallpox outbreak that had occurred along its banks: *chickamauga* translates as "river of death." By September 18, Bragg hoped to force Rosecrans's hand by placing himself between the Yankees and Chattanooga. The movement precipitated a major battle that resulted in an enormous Confederate victory.

The battle erupted on September 19 at Jay's Mill and spread south to a point near Lee and Gordon's Mill. The fields, cabins, and woods in the area witnessed repeated, rolling attacks that washed over the same ground, resulting in gains that were mostly temporary. Kelly Field, Brock Field, the Poe Cabin, Viniard Field, the Winfrey House, and Alexander's Bridge all gained a measure of instant fame in the day's dreadful action. The battle was renewed the next day. Again

George Brotherton Cabin, Chickamauga, Georgia

On September 19, 1863, William Rosecrans's Union force engaged Confederates commanded by Braxton Bragg near a little creek called Chickamauga. The decisive Confederate attack of September 20 by James Longstreet's corps enveloped the ground around George Brotherton's cabin.

Bragg stabbed toward Chattanooga, inciting engagements along the entire north-south battle line. The fearful fighting produced unspectacular results until timing struck just right: Union brigadier general Thomas J. Wood was ordered to move his division to support another area, creating a quarter-mile-wide gap in the Federal line. Nearly at this moment, Longstreet sent six divisions forward, plowing through the Yankees and rolling them back in startled confusion. It was one of the great frontal attacks of the war.

"Now the enemy are in plain view along the road covering our entire front," James R. Carnahan, a captain in the 86th Indiana Infantry, wrote of the attack. "You can see them, as with cap visors drawn well down over their eyes, the gun at the charge, with short, shrill shouts they come, and we see the colors of Longstreet's corps, flushed with victory, confronting us." On the Confederate side, Captain William Miller Owen, a staff officer of Brigadier General William Preston's, recorded his impression of the attack: "The men rush over the hastily-constructed breastworks of logs and rails of the foe, with the old time familiar

Lee and Gordon's Mill photographed in 1863.

National Archives and Records Administration

Lee and Gordon's Mill, Chickamauga

The southernmost part of the Chickamauga battle-field saw little action, but skirmishes flared around a prominent structure, Lee and Gordon's Mill. Situated on Chickamauga Creek, the building has recently been reconstructed and enlarged.

Bronze Field Piece, Viniard Field, Chickamauga

Union artillery was employed in heavy action at Chickamauga. This bronze field piece, located in Viniard Field, bears the muzzle inscription "Fired 1000 Rounds / 1842." Evidently it was a veteran long before the Civil War began.

rebel yell, and, wheeling then to the right, the column sweeps the enemy before it, and pushes along the Chattanooga road towards Missionary Ridge in pursuit. It is glorious!"[22]

Pushed to a series of hills northwest of the center of the field, the last remnants held fast to a region called Horseshoe Ridge, which included Snodgrass Hill and a little cabinlike house owned by George Washington Snodgrass. The Rebs had the Yankees on the run, and only Major General George H. Thomas and the remainder of the Federal army held the ground here, earning Thomas the sobriquet "Rock of Chickamauga." It was a desperate day, but Thomas's resistance prevented a rout and allowed Rosecrans and the bulk of the Union army to scurry back to Chattanooga. Of the action on the hill, Lieutenant Colonel Gates P. Thruston, a Federal staff officer, recalled: "The Union line held the crest. Longstreet was stayed at last. Gathering new forces, he soon sent a flanking column around our right. We could not extend our line to meet this attack. . . . For a time the fate of the Union army hung in the balance. All seemed lost, when unexpected help came from Gordon Granger and the right was saved."[23]

The battle was a Union disaster and a spectacular, albeit brief, Confederate return to domination. Chickamauga caused such panic in Washington that Lincoln sparked an enormous movement to reinforce Rosecrans's apparently stunned and mauled army. The new star, Grant, would personally supervise the rebuilding of the force, now pinned in Chattanooga and running out of food and supplies. The situation was desperate. A week after Chickamauga, Kate Cumming, a Confederate nurse, recorded her impressions of the wounded left behind: "As we rode out of the yard, I tried to look neither to the right nor the left, for I knew that

John Ross House, Rossville, Georgia

Major General Gordon Granger played an oblique role at Chickamauga, commanding the Union reserve corps. Granger established headquarters at the John Ross House, home of the principal chief of the Cherokee Nation. It was since moved and partly rebuilt.

13th Michigan Infantry Monument, Chickamauga

In Viniard Field the 13th Michigan Infantry fought savagely against a battle line of Confederates from Texas, Arkansas, and Florida. The 13th Michigan was commanded by Colonel Joshua B. Culver.

many eyes were sadly gazing at us from their comfortless sheds and tents. I could do nothing for the poor fellows, and when that is the case, I try to steel my heart against their sorrows."[24]

Chattanooga now became the focus of the autumn of the war's middle year. The reinforcements sent to the Federals in Chattanooga included troops of Major Generals Joseph Hooker and William Tecumseh Sherman, and by October Grant

124th Ohio Infantry Monument, Brock Field, Chickamauga

Brock Field was the scene of heavy and repeated fighting throughout the battle and was the starting point for Longstreet's major attack. The 124th Ohio Infantry Monument remembers the regiment commanded by Colonel Oliver Payne.

was in town taking charge. Starving and surrounded, the Yankees opened a tenuous "cracker line" of supplies from Bridgeport, Alabama, across a peninsula of land called Moccasin Point alongside the Tennessee River. Bragg's victorious Confederates held the high ground: Lookout Mountain to the south and Missionary Ridge to the east. The river bordered the town on the west and north. Along the Confederate lines, picket duty was tense. Joseph B. Polley, a soldier in Hood's Texas Brigade, wrote: "All too soon the dreaded and fateful hour arrived; all too soon the whisper order 'Forward' was passed from man to man down the long line, and, like spectral forms in the ghastly moonlight, the Confederate pickets moved slowly out into the open field in their front, every moment expecting to see the flash of a gun and hear or feel its messenger of death." [25]

Bragg's army was not well supplied and, despite the victory at Chickamauga, lacked confidence in its commanding general. Thomas attacked and captured Orchard Knob, a hill midway between the river and Missionary Ridge, on November 23. The following day, Hooker's men assaulted and captured Lookout Mountain. The attack succeeded partly because of a blinding fog that gave the action the name "battle above the clouds," but mostly because the greater part of the Confederate troops had been withdrawn. On November 25, Bragg concentrated

Moccasin Point from Lookout Mountain, Chattanooga

With Grant in command, the Union forces hemmed in at Chattanooga managed to open a supply line across this narrow neck of land in a cutback of the Tennessee River.

Lookout Mountain from Chattanooga National Cemetery

Beaten and entrapped in Chattanooga, the Federal army was in desperate straits in late September. Bragg laid siege to the city occupying Missionary Ridge and Lookout Mountain (background).

Snodgrass Hill, Chickamauga *(left)*

Broken by Longstreet's push, Rosecrans and most of his army fled north toward Chattanooga. On Snodgrass Hill, Brigadier General George H. Thomas made a stand that prevented a total Union rout.

his army on Missionary Ridge. Capturing that position would require a herculean effort. As the bulk of the Federal army fanned into several attack points under the ridge, casualties mounted. Sherman's boys assaulted the northern position but stalled at Tunnel Hill. Samuel H. M. Byers, a first lieutenant in the 5th Iowa Infantry, was captured near the railroad tunnel. "In a moment I reflected that I was a prisoner," he recalled, "and horrible pictures of Libby and Andersonville flashed through my mind—and with them the presentiment of evil I had had the night before the assault."[26]

Just when the Union attack seemed desperately checked, one of the spectacular events of the war occurred. Thomas's men, ordered to go from Orchard Knob to the base of Missionary Ridge and capture the enemy rifle pits, did so—and then, after a pause, proceeded up the mountain. The Federal high command, watching from Orchard Knob, was stunned. It was a soldier's battle in the truest sense as waves of blue coated the mountain and slowly captured the Confederate guns high atop its crest. "This, I confess, staggered me," wrote Major James A. Connolly. "I couldn't understand it; it looked as though we were going to assault

Robert Cravens House, Lookout Mountain

On November 24 revitalized Yankee soldiers scaled and captured Lookout Mountain, aided largely by a Confederate withdrawal. The Robert Cravens House, halfway up the mountain, had served as Confederate brigadier general Edward C. Walthall's headquarters. Soldiers called it the "White House on the Bench."

the Ridge. 'Charge' is shouted wildly from hundreds of throats, and with a yell such as that valley never heard before, the three divisions rushed forward. Our men, stirred by some memories, shouted 'Chickamauga!' as they scaled the works at the summit." [27]

Bragg had no choice but to retreat into Georgia. The movement opened up the possibility for Sherman's invasion of the state, the Atlanta campaign, and the March to the Sea that would follow. Federal troops now firmly occupied Chattanooga and controlled its railroads and communications. "The disaster admits of no palliation, and is justly disparaging to me as a commander," wrote Bragg, in a letter to Jefferson Davis. "I trust, however, you may find on full investigation that the fault is not entirely mine." [28]

The war of 1863 was rapidly coming to a close. As the armies clashed at Chattanooga, other events occurred in eastern Tennessee at Knoxville, where Longstreet had been sent following Chickamauga, partly because of his animosity toward Bragg. Eastern Tennessee, with its pro-Union sentiment, had long been a

Orchard Knob, Chattanooga

A day before the capture of Lookout Mountain, soldiers under George Thomas "drilled" in sight of their Confederate counterparts. As the drill unfolded, however, they fought their way eastward to capture Orchard Knob, a strategic position that afforded a command post for Grant during the final days of the Chattanooga campaign.

Missionary Ridge, Chattanooga *(overleaf)*

On November 25 a major Union attack unfolded toward Missionary Ridge, the commanding position east of Chattanooga. The initiative of George Thomas's men, who took their assigned objective at the foot of the ridge and then kept right on going, pushed the Confederate defenders away. Guns like these of Captain Robert Cobb's Kentucky battery could not be trained low enough to fire at the oncoming Yankees as they attacked straight uphill.

The afternoon of the Gettysburg Address: This image was made on November 19, 1863, and shows the crowd gathered for the dedication of the Soldier's National Cemetery. The Evergreen Cemetery Gatehouse is faintly visible on the left horizon.

Library of Congress

Soldier's National Monument, Gettysburg

Erected in 1869, the Soldier's National Monument dominates Gettysburg National Cemetery. In addition to marking the resting place of 3,629 soldiers, the shaft was intended to stand on the position from which Lincoln delivered the Gettysburg Address. Lincoln's platform actually stood on or near the Brown family vault in nearby Evergreen Cemetery.

problem for the Confederacy, and Longstreet wished to attack Major General Ambrose E. Burnside's Yankees operating in the region. Small actions erupted before Burnside retreated into Knoxville, pursued by Longstreet. A microsiege unfolded before Longstreet attacked Fort Sanders on November 29. A deep, icy ditch prevented Confederate success. "For fully twenty minutes the men stood around the ditch unable to get at their adversaries but unwilling to retreat," wrote Colonel Edward Porter Alexander, Longstreet's acting chief of artillery. Captain Orlando M. Poe, Burnside's chief engineer, recalled, "Meanwhile those who remained in the ditch found themselves under a deadly flank fire of musketry and canister, supplemented by shells thrown as hand-grenades from inside the fort, without the slightest possibility of returning a blow."[29] The Confederate attack failed, and Longstreet was ordered back to support the Army of Northern Virginia.

Before the year ended, the United States president solidified the sense of purpose brought into the war the previous New Year's Day. For his trip to Gettysburg to dedicate the new National Cemetery, Lincoln struggled to express the meaning of all the death, the suffering, the smoke and battle. On November 19, speaking for little more than two minutes after the two-hour oration of Edward Everett, Lincoln concluded: "It is rather for us to be here dedicated to the great task remaining before us—that from these honored dead we take increased devotion to that cause for which they gave the last full measure of devotion—that we here highly resolve that these dead shall not have died in vain—that this nation, under God, shall have a new birth of freedom—and that government of the people, by the people, for the people shall not perish from the Earth."[30]

THE YANKEES PENETRATE THE SOUTHLAND

The nature of the war would change considerably during 1864. No longer would the Confederacy feel such confidence in its ability to outlast the conviction of the North or to win support from foreign powers. Never again would the eastern Confederate army bring the war onto northern soil, apart from small-scale raids. Now diminishing supplies and an increasingly harder life for citizens on the home front would begin to plague the decision making of Confederate commanders. And the Union victory at Chattanooga would allow a Yankee penetration deep into the Southland that would endanger the Confederates' ability to continue waging war.

During the final weeks of 1863, the eastern armies under Lee and Meade had engaged in a fruitless exercise known as the Mine Run campaign. Lee's army, somewhat scattered, constructed quarters south of the Rapidan River to serve as winter lodging. Meade's plan of attack was not executed well, and by the opening days of December both armies sat inactive, resigned to the harsh weather.

After Lincoln's ongoing frustrations with the eastern commanders, U. S. Grant's successive victories in the West did not go unnoticed. Lincoln appointed Grant general in chief of all armies in the field and commissioned him lieutenant general in the regular army, the first use of that grade since George Washington. Now Grant would direct all military operations, save for those of the navy, and he would have little to do with his old comrade Henry W. Halleck, whose role was now rather like a chief of staff, in Washington. Warned to avoid the capital by his good friend William T. Sherman, Grant determined to establish his headquarters in the field, where politicians couldn't meddle with him. He would accompany Meade and the Army of the Potomac.

With winter at hand and the Rapidan River separating the eastern armies, even the active Grant could accomplish little for the moment. A number of relatively small engagements took place farther south and west, however. In Mississippi, Sherman launched the Meridian expedition to destroy railroads and military resources in the central portion of the state—something of a dress rehearsal for his March to the Sea later the same year. On February 3 he moved from Vicksburg with 25,000 men. They faced scattered forces under four Confederate commanders. After five skirmishes Sherman's army wrecked the facilities at Meridian before returning to Vicksburg.

As Sherman was busily ruining the military value of Meridian, the largest battle of the war fought in Florida occurred. At Olustee, Brigadier General Truman Seymour's Federals clashed with Confederates under Brigadier General Joseph Finegan. A relatively small engagement, the battle nonetheless ended as a spectacular Confederate victory, with heavy losses to Seymour's Yankees. On the same day, the war in northern Georgia accelerated. Since the Union occupation of Chattanooga, Confederate general Joseph E. Johnston had positioned forces around Dalton, Georgia. A reconnaissance on February 22 by Union major general John M. Palmer checked the enemy's positions and produced clashes at Tun-

Fort Pillow, Tennessee

Confederate cavalry under Brigadier General James R. Chalmers attacked the garrison at Fort Pillow on April 12, 1864. The occupying force consisted of 262 black and 295 white soldiers. Major General Nathan Bedford Forrest arrived; 231 Yankee soldiers were killed, many as they surrendered or even after they threw down their arms, and the episode remains controversial.

nel Hill, Rocky Face Ridge, and Varnell's Station. It was an approach that would be fought over far more heavily in the weeks to come.

The possible Confederate recapture of Arkansas and Louisiana continued to worry the Lincoln administration—that concern was the primary reason for Sherman's Meridian expedition. Lincoln also worried over the French governance of Mexico and desired a strong show of Federal force in Texas. He therefore acquiesced to Halleck's request to launch a series of operations that became known as the Red River campaign. This befuddled series of maneuvers, led by Major General Nathaniel P. Banks, was to be coordinated with Sherman and Major General Frederick Steele. It was a combined operation, with naval gunboats under Rear Admiral David D. Porter providing support.

The campaign lasted until May 18, produced a large series of small skirmishes and a few battles, and saw Porter's gunboats entrapped by low water on the Red River near Alexandria, Louisiana. It ended with virtually nothing accomplished but a great deal of disarray on both sides. Perhaps the brightest spot in the whole affair was the ingenuity displayed by Union engineer Joseph Bailey in saving Porter's flotilla. On May 16 Porter wrote from his flagship, *Black Hawk,* to Navy Secretary Gideon Welles: "I have the honor to inform you that the vessels lately caught by low water above the falls at Alexandria, have been released from their unpleasant position. . . . Lieut.-Colonel Bailey, Acting Engineer of the 19th Army Corps, proposed a plan of building a series of dams across the rocks at the falls, and raising the water high enough to let the vessels pass over." [1]

Apart from the participants in these lesser campaigns, most men on both sides survived as best they could through the long winter and wondered about the desperate battles sure to come. Religion filled the lives of an increasing number of soldiers in 1864, as the war dragged on and on. "The church was very neat and filled with soldiers, but one woman in the audience," wrote Jenkin Jones of the 6th Wisconsin Artillery, at church in Huntsville, Alabama, on January 17. "Chaplain of 18th Wisconsin officiated, of the Calvinistic school, and but ill agreed with my views, but it seemed good to be once more listening to an earnest speaker and hear the old-fashioned tunes swell in the bass voices that filled the room. Returned to camp, if not better a more thoughtful man." Another Federal soldier, Theodore Upson of the 100th Indiana Infantry, in Bellefont, Alabama, tried to reassure his parents about army life: "I have had several letters from the home people asking me about drinking in the Army, and Father has written me saying he hopes I am not getting to be a d[r]unkard as he hears many of the soldiers are. I think you good people at home must imagine we keep a barrel of whisky on tap all of the time. . . . Do not worry, Father mine, I am not going to the dogs." [2]

In the Army of Northern Virginia, meanwhile, the tone was becoming grim. "Short rations are having a bad effect upon the men, both morally and physically," wrote Robert E. Lee to War Secretary James A. Seddon on January 22. "Desertions to the enemy are becoming more frequent, and the men cannot continue healthy and vigorous if confined to this spare diet for any length of time. Unless there is a change, I fear the army cannot be kept together." Perhaps because the outlook for them was growing bleak, southern soldiers turned to religion even more avidly than their northern counterparts. "If this state of things should continue for any considerable length of time, we will have in the Army of Tennessee an army of believers," wrote T. J. Stokes, who was possibly chaplain of the 10th Texas Infantry, near Dalton, Georgia, on April 18. "Does the history of the world record anywhere the like? Even Cromwell's time sinks into insignificance. A revival so vast in its proportions, and under all the difficulties attending camp life, that bad weather this spring, and innumerable difficulties, is certainly an earnest of better, brighter times not far in the future."[3]

In the East, the armies were positioning themselves for what might be the decisive campaign of the war. The Federals now had a commanding general who understood fully that the issue was not geography, but destruction of the enemy armies and their ability to wage war. "Lee's army will be your objective point," wrote Grant from Culpeper Court House on April 9 to George G. Meade. "Wherever Lee goes, there you will go also."[4] By the first days of May, with the onset of warm weather, Grant's 119,000 men were spread north of the Rapidan from Culpeper Court House to Manassas Junction. Lee's 64,000 lay south of the river from Gordonsville to near the Wilderness, with Stuart's cavalry south of Fredericksburg. Lee's position could not be attacked frontally. Grant would need to turn Lee's right to preserve his line of communications and threaten Lee's. So on May 3 he ordered the army corps under Major Generals Winfield Scott Hancock, John Sedgwick, and Gouverneur K. Warren south to Germanna Ford and Ely's Ford on the river, where they would cross and move into the Wilderness.

Just after midnight on May 4 Hancock's 2d Army Corps and Warren's 5th Army corps crossed the fords and moved into the Wilderness, unsupported by artillery or cavalry. Grant hoped to move the men through the brushy, heavily wooded region quickly, but by early afternoon Warren had halted at Wilderness Tavern and Hancock near Chancellorsville. Meanwhile, Confederates under Lieutenant General Richard S. Ewell were approaching Warren by the Orange-Fredericksburg Turnpike and those under Lieutenant General A. P. Hill were approaching Hancock on the Orange Plank Road. Longstreet was approaching too, but farther behind. "You will already have learned that the army of Gen Meade is in motion, and is crossing the Rapidan on our right, whether with the intention of attacking, or moving towards Fredericksburg, I am not able to say," Lee wrote Jefferson Davis on May 4. "But it is apparent that the long threatened effort to take Richmond has begun, and that the enemy has collected all his available force to accomplish it."[5]

On the morning of May 5, Ewell clashed with Warren, opening the battle of the Wilderness. Sedgwick arrived from the north, supporting Warren with three additional divisions, and Hancock approached from Todd's Tavern. The

Drewry's Bluff, Virginia

During early May 1864 Grant initiated a campaign that would force Lee back toward Richmond. Major General Benjamin F. Butler conducted a simultaneous operation on the James River and fought near Drewry's Bluff, the main Confederate fortification downriver from Richmond. Retracing the route of Richmond-bound ships, the Annabel Lee *passes within cannon range of the fort.*

Yankees, spread along a northwest-southeast line across the Orange Turnpike, faced the five divisions of Ewell and Hill. The poor visibility in the Wilderness and the difficulty of holding formations meant that attackers were normally heard well before they could fire on the defenders. Confederate troops seemed better adapted to the woods, and the Federals were relying on poor maps. Moreover, Confederate attacks in such conditions were especially unnerving to the Yankees, due to the fearsome Rebel yell. "The Federal, or 'Yankee,' yell, compared with that of the Confederate, lacked in vocal breadth, pitch, and resonance," explained Harvie Dew of the 9th Virginia Cavalry. "This was unquestionably attributable to the fact that the soldiery of the North was drawn and recruited chiefly from large cities and towns, from factory districts, and from the more densely settled portions of the country."

"In an instant every voice with one accord vigorously shouted that 'Rebel yell,'" Dew continued, "which was so often heard on the field of battle. 'Woh-who-ey! who-ey! who-ey! Woh-oh-ey! who-ey! etc. (The best illustration of this 'true yell' which can be given the reader is by spelling it as above, with directions to sound the first syllable 'woh' short and low, and the second 'who' with a very high and prolonged note deflecting upon the third syllable, 'ey.')"[6]

The Confederates worked the psychological advantages well, and because of various hesitations on the Federals' part, they held their lines in strong fashion until darkness fell. Each army planned an attack for the next morning. Longstreet was ordered to attack the Federal right. At 5 A.M. on May 6, much of the Federal line lunged forward on the offensive, with Ewell defending well on the north and Hill, to the south, breaking in confusion. As the Confederate right was crumbling, Longstreet arrived and reinforced the position. On the northern-

Ellwood, Wilderness, Virginia

On May 5–7 the Army of the Potomac and the Army of Northern Virginia fought a savage battle in the Wilderness. The J. Horace Lacy House, Ellwood, served as Major General Gouverneur K. Warren's headquarters during the battle; here Grant and Meade discussed strategy.

Wilderness Tavern

Lee's attack from the south during the first day at the Wilderness inflicted heavy casualties at several Union positions, including at the Wilderness Tavern. Only the remains of a chimney belonging to one of the tavern's outbuildings stand today.

most end of the line, Brigadier General John B. Gordon launched a Confederate attack that succeeded until halted by darkness. On May 7 the armies reinforced their lines and mostly stayed inactive, with fires consuming parts of the Wilderness brush that separated them—fires that burned some wounded to death. The casualties were heavy, amounting to possibly as many as 30,000 total. And neither side had gained a meaningful outcome. But rather than retreat, Grant chose to turn Lee's left and race toward Richmond, forcing the Confederate commander to block him at the junction of roads near Spotsylvania Court House.

On May 8, as elements of both armies vied for position near Spotsylvania, Warren's infantry clashed with Confederate units of Longstreet's corps, now commanded by Major General Richard H. Anderson—Longstreet having been seriously wounded, accidentally, by his own men, on the Brock Road two days earlier. A Federal attack late in the afternoon was too poorly coordinated to achieve a significant result. On May 9 the Confederate corps of Anderson, Ewell, and Major General Jubal A. Early (temporarily replacing A. P. Hill, who was sick) formed in a semicircle near Spotsylvania Court House, the Federals approaching from the northwest (Hancock, Warren, and Sedgwick) and from the northeast (Major General Ambrose E. Burnside). On this day, as aides worried over his exposure to Confederate fire, Sedgwick was killed, hit below the left eye by a Minié bullet. Among his last words were, "They couldn't hit an elephant at this distance."

The following day the Confederate line tightened and part of Ewell's position formed a salient that came to be called the "Mule Shoe" around the McCoull and

15th New Jersey Infantry Monument, Spotsylvania Court House, Virginia

The 15th New Jersey Monument stands at the site of the so-called Bloody Angle, where some of the most intense fighting of the war took place during the Spotsylvania campaign.

Confederate Cemetery, Spotsylvania Court House

At Spotsylvania, the Confederate Cemetery holds some 600 soldiers killed during the fighting there and nearby.

Harrison houses. Grant had the opportunity to turn Lee's left but determined on a frontal assault led by Hancock. At 4 P.M. on May 10, Hancock, Warren, and Major General Horatio G. Wright (having replaced Sedgwick) struck vigorously into Anderson's corps. The resulting casualties were monstrous. "Ambulances and army wagons with two tiers of flooring, loaded with wounded and drawn by four and six mule teams, pass along the plank, or rather, corduroy road to Fredericksburg," wrote Augustus Brown of the 4th New York Heavy Artillery. "Many of the wounds are full of maggots. I saw one man with an arm off at the shoulder, with maggots half an inch long crawling in the sloughing flesh, and several poor fellows were holding stumps of legs and arms straight up in the air so as to ease the pain the road and the heartless drivers subjected them to."[7]

May 11 was quiet, masking a grim determination on Grant's part to engineer the end of the war. "I propose to fight it out on this line, if it takes all summer," he wrote Henry Halleck that day. All knew that the heavy fighting in what was becoming a minisiege would continue. "I shall come out of this fight a live major general or a dead brigadier," wrote Brigadier General Abner Monroe Perrin, who commanded a brigade in A. P. Hill's corps.[8] He was killed the next day. On May 12 a vicious frontal attack by Hancock plunged into the Mule Shoe, giving rise to the name Bloody Angle for the apex of the line, and attacks and counterattacks continued until dusk. The fighting was stubborn, and Lee slowly began to develop a new line south of the Mule Shoe.

Union cavalry under Major General Philip H. Sheridan had been undertaking a raid on Richmond, drawing Jeb Stuart away from Lee's army. The approach to Richmond culminated in the battle of Yellow Tavern, where Stuart was mortally wounded on May 11, dying the next day. After destroying supplies and railroad,

Sheridan returned to Grant's army on May 24. After continued fighting around Spotsylvania Court House, Grant again threatened Lee's strategic interests by sending Hancock to Guinea's Station and interposing Federal forces between Lee's army and Richmond. A rush to the next line of defenses ensued for Lee, who withdrew to the North Anna River. After a fight on May 23 both armies again raced southward, Lee's army arriving astride the old battlefields of the Peninsula campaign of 1862 by May 28. Elements of Grant's army arrived east of Atlee's Station and Cold Harbor on May 30 and June 1.

At Cold Harbor, Lee's army of about 59,000 faced Grant's force of about 108,000. Between Richmond and Petersburg, Major General Benjamin F. Butler's Army of the James, consisting of 14,600 men, faced P. G. T. Beauregard's 9,000 Confederates. Sheridan had established a position at Old Cold Harbor, and Lee planned to take the offensive. He sent Anderson to strike Sheridan, but with disastrous results: the Confederates scattered in retreat. The next day, both armies moved toward Cold Harbor. In the early morning of June 3, Grant ordered a frontal attack designed to push Lee to the Chickahominy, but more than 7,000 Yankee soldiers were cut down in less than one hour. "The dead and dying lay in

Confederate Trenches at Cold Harbor, Virginia

At Cold Harbor on June 3, Lee's heavily entrenched Confederates threw back head-on attacks by Grant that cost more than 7,000 Union soldiers in less than an hour. Earthworks along the line, although much eroded, remain visible.

front of the Confederate lines in triangles, of which the apexes were the bravest men who came nearest to the breastworks under the withering, deadly fire," wrote Charles Venable, a staff officer of Lee's. The armies dug in and stubbornly fought from the trenches for the next nine days, the cost in suffering and casualties fearful. "We are now at Cold Harbor, where we have been since June 1," wrote Federal colonel Emory Upton on June 5. "On that day we had a murderous engagement. I say murderous, because we were recklessly ordered to assault the enemy's intrenchments, knowing neither their strength nor position. Our loss was very heavy, and to no purpose. Our men are brave, but cannot accomplish impossibilities." Despite the savage fighting and the newspaper reports of monstrous casualties, young men were still eager to support both armies with their sweat and blood. Richard Corbin, a young southerner in Paris, ran the blockade to join his beloved army. "*Veni,* Vici, and as Julius Caesar remarked, we have gone in and won," he wrote on June 5, from Wilmington. "Thank Heaven I am at last on Confederate soil, having most successfully passed through that awful ordeal . . . the blockade."[9]

On June 12 Grant initiated a movement that would set up the final months of the war. He would shift his base of operations south of the James River, capture Petersburg, and threaten the last railroad connecting Richmond with the outside world. To do this, he established a second line at Cold Harbor and withdrew under the cover of darkness, sending Major General William F. Smith's 18th Corps to Bermuda Hundred, where it arrived on June 14–15. The remaining corps also sped southward, and by the time Lee discovered what he thought was happening, he simply moved Anderson and A. P. Hill south toward Malvern Hill to block an approach toward Richmond. Grant had fooled Lee entirely.

Eppes House, Appomattox Manor, City Point, Virginia

On June 15 Grant established headquarters at City Point at the confluence of the James and Appomattox Rivers. Over the following ten months the spot would become the busiest seaport in the world, with supplies coming in just seven miles from Petersburg. The spacious Eppes house, Appomattox Manor, was given to Grant's chief quartermaster, Brigadier General Rufus Ingalls.

Grant ordered Smith to attack and capture Petersburg at daybreak on June 15. But Smith approached cautiously and reconnoitered the city's defenses extensively, so that the attack was not launched until 7 P.M. The Federals captured two redans with ease, and by the fall of darkness nothing prevented them from marching straight into Petersburg. Smith, however, concerned about possible growing Confederate strength in the area, decided to stay put until he was reinforced. The opportunity was lost. On June 16 heavy reinforcements arrived, along with Grant, who ordered an attack at 6 P.M. that resulted in the capture of a portion of the Confederate line. A light attack on the following day and a heavy assault on June 18 failed against the strengthening Confederate defenses. "I shall never forget the hurricane of shot and shell which struck us as we emerged from the belt of trees," wrote Augustus Brown of the battle on June 18. "The sound of the whizzing bullets and exploding shells, blending in awful volume, seemed like the terrific hissing of some gigantic furnace. Men, torn and bleeding, fell headlong from the ranks as the murderous hail swept through the line."[10] The Petersburg operations were transforming into a siege. Indeed, sporadic fighting around a deepening network of trenches would characterize the remainder of the war on the Petersburg front—punctuated by infrequent major attacks.

Grant's City Point cabin photographed from the rear in 1864 or 1865. Note the waving flag and the privy.

Library of Congress

While these many developments were transforming the character of the war in Virginia, Major General William T. Sherman was transforming war itself in Georgia. In May, Sherman, who commanded the Military Division of the Mississippi, moved his three armies southward toward the Army of Tennessee, commanded by General Joseph E. Johnston. Sherman brought the Army of the Ten-

Kennesaw Mountain, Georgia

The western theater was alive with action in mid-1864. Major General William T. Sherman worked his way south from Chattanooga during the early months; by June 27 he attacked headlong into the Confederate defenses at Kennesaw Mountain.

Union trenches near the base of Kennesaw Mountain photographed in 1864 by George N. Barnard.

National Archives and Records Administration

nessee (24,000 men commanded by Major General James B. McPherson), the Army of the Cumberland (61,000 under Major General George H. Thomas), and the Army of the Ohio (13,500 under Major General John M. Schofield) against some 50,000 of Johnston's defenders. Sherman's goals were to crush Johnston's army, move against the rail center of Atlanta, and destroy the heart of Georgia's capacity to support wartime operations.

The armies clashed at Rocky Face Ridge on May 5–7. On May 13 Johnston fell back to Resaca, hoping to lure Sherman into a foolish attack. Elements of the armies clashed at this position for three days before Johnston again pulled back, allowing Sherman to capture the manufacturing town of Rome. After additional skirmishing, Johnston retreated to the heavily defended position of Allatoona Pass. During May 25–27 the armies clashed at Dallas, and Sherman continued turning movements that forced Johnston southward toward Atlanta. Union soldiers established a supply depot at Big Shanty—the position from which Andrews's raid had departed two years before—and by late June, Johnston constructed a heavy defensive line along Kennesaw Mountain, northwest of Marietta. There, on June 27, a savage frontal assault from Sherman resulted in bloody casualties, particularly for the Union attackers, who amassed 3,000 killed, wounded, and missing.

The armies of Sherman and Johnston contrasted starkly to those of the East. They were largely made up of western and midwestern men, many of whom had a rough, rugged character. Yet they were all simply Americans, and not all intently devoted to military protocol. "With regard to the general appearance of the Westerners, it is not so different from our own as I had supposed, but certain it is that discipline is most astonishingly lax," wrote Federal staff officer John Chipman Gray that summer.[11] Lax discipline or not, the Yankees continued moving south. Johnston next dug in along the Chattahoochie River, where again Sherman turned his line, forcing a withdrawal to Peachtree Creek on July 9. For a week, Sherman prepared for a major, coordinated movement across the river. Meanwhile, Jefferson Davis had reached the limits of his tolerance with Joe Johnston, whose repeated movements southward initiated a near panic in the Confederate capital. Johnston's replacement, assigned on July 17, was Lieutenant General John Bell Hood, veteran of many battles that among other things had left him without his right leg (lost at Chickamauga) and the use of his left arm (at Gettysburg). Now he would attempt to defend the heart of the rail system supporting the Deep South.

Hood defended Atlanta with the corps of Lieutenant General William J. Hardee and Major Generals Benjamin F. Cheatham and Alexander P. Stewart. In the battle of Peachtree Creek on July 20, Hood attacked Thomas and suffered heavy casualties. He then backed into the defenses of Atlanta. The battle of Atlanta came two days later. McPherson was killed in the fighting. On July 28 Major General Oliver O. Howard, who had replaced McPherson, pushed north-

Illinois Monument, Cheatham Hill, Kennesaw Mountain

The Illinois Monument at Cheatham Hill marks the position where, along a salient in the Confederate lines, the most savage fighting of the battle occurred. The monument was constructed above an unfinished tunnel begun by Union soldiers to explode powder under the Rebel position.

Peter Kolb Farm, Kennesaw Mountain

A few days before the main attack at Kennesaw Mountain, John Bell Hood's Confederates smashed into the Yankee line at Peter Kolb's farm, used by Joseph Hooker as a headquarters and now preserved as an elegant cabin.

westward around the city and toward Ezra Church, where he attempted to cut the rail lines but was unsuccessful. A detachment of cavalry left on a mission to free Union prisoners at Andersonville, far to the south, but was itself captured. Sherman finally advanced on August 26, and Hood's groggy response led to the battle of Jonesboro, south of Atlanta, on August 30–September 1. Hood pulled out of Atlanta in the late afternoon of September 1, and Federal troops marched in, escorting civilians out of the area and converting the city into a fortified supply camp. "You cannot qualify war in harsher terms than I will," Sherman wrote Atlanta's mayor, James M. Calhoun, on September 12. "War is cruelty, and you cannot refine it. . . . You might as well appeal against the thunder-storm as against these terrible hardships of war."[12] Hood scattered northward into a campaign of pure folly.

Elsewhere, a variety of land and naval actions marked the summer of 1864. On June 10 at Brice's Crossroads, Mississippi, Confederate cavalry great Nathan Bedford Forrest, now a major general, defeated Federal major general Samuel D. Sturgis's force of 7,800 with less than half that number. The war touched Europe

Atlanta from Kennesaw Mountain

Atlanta lies on the horizon as seen from the summit of Kennesaw Mountain. Following the battle, Sherman resumed flanking movements, crossed the Chattahoochie River on July 9, and closed in on the city, capturing it on September 2.

14th New Jersey Infantry Monument, Monocacy, Maryland

When Jubal Early brought his Rebel army to the doorstep of Washington, resistance by Lew Wallace's troops along the Monocacy River bought precious time for the capital city. The 14th New Jersey Infantry Monument stands guard over the memory of the dead.

when on June 19 the USS *Kearsarge* battled with the CSS *Alabama,* the notorious raider that had sunk, burned, or captured 69 ships. Off the coast of Cherbourg, France, the *Kearsarge,* commanded by Captain John A. Winslow, sank Captain Raphael Semmes's *Alabama.* In the Shenandoah Valley on June 23, Confederate major general Jubal A. Early began a raid that would bring the terror of war to the outskirts of Washington City. On July 2 Early's 10,000 infantry and 4,000 cavalry arrived at Winchester, and the Federal army picked up the offensive movement. Early was checked by Major General Lew Wallace along the Monocacy River near Frederick, Maryland, on July 9. Although this battle stopped Early's advance only briefly, it allowed the Union defenses of Washington to tighten. On July 11–12 Early made his closest pass to the capital when he skirmished at Fort Stevens, a battle briefly witnessed by President Lincoln.

The focus, however, remained on the Petersburg defense lines, where the tedium of trench warfare ground on. "I have only one earthly want," Robert E. Lee wrote his son Custis, "that God in His infinite mercy will send our enemies back to their homes."[13] Grant had no such intention, however. The frustrating stalemate at Petersburg had led to an idea from a regiment of Pennsylvania coal miners—to tunnel underneath the Confederate works, pack the tunnel with black powder, and blow a breach in the line so that troops could rush through to victory. Lieutenant Colonel Henry Pleasants of the 48th Pennsylvania Infantry received permission to proceed with the plan, and by July 23 a shaft measuring 511 feet long extended to a position some 20 feet below the Confederate line. Federal soldiers placed some four tons of black powder—some 320 kegs—into the mine adit.

Confederates had detected the operation and constructed a smaller countermine but had no indication of the impending explosion. It came at 4:45 A.M. on July 30. The blast formed a crater 170 feet long, 60 to 80 feet wide, and 30 feet deep. Nine companies of Confederate soldiers were hurled into the air, and some

"The Dictator" (Replica), Petersburg, Virginia

In Grant's protracted siege of Petersburg, one of the workhorses of the Union artillery was "The Dictator," a 13-inch seacoast mortar that lobbed 200-pound shells nearly a mile into the Confederate lines. "The Dictator" itself probably resides on the state capitol grounds in Hartford, Connecticut.

"The Dictator" on a flatcar photographed outside the Petersburg lines by David Knox in 1864.

Library of Congress

278 of the men were killed instantly. In the ensuing melee, confused tactics resulted when Union soldiers became mired into the debris rather than pushing forward. Two officers commanding the attack, Brigadier Generals Edward Ferrero and James H. Ledlie, cowered in a bombproof, drinking liquor. It was one of the great disasters of the war. After the smoke, the destruction, and the death, nothing had changed—the Petersburg siege continued.

* * *

Union Mine Entrance, Petersburg

Starting at this point, a Union regiment made up largely of coal miners tunneled under the Rebel lines and packed the tunnel with gunpowder beneath the Confederate battery in Elliott's Salient.

Far to the southwest, near Mobile, Alabama, a Federal naval force commanded by Rear Admiral David G. Farragut prepared to cut off one of the Confederacy's remaining major ports. In addition to his flagship, the USS *Hartford,* Farragut's force consisted of four monitors and thirteen wooden ships. He faced the ironclad ram CSS *Tennessee* and three gunboats, the CSS *Morgan,* CSS *Gaines,* and CSS *Selma,* commanded by Admiral Franklin Buchanan. At 6 A.M. on August 5 Farragut commenced, attempting to run the guns of Forts Morgan, Gaines, and Powell. The heavy guns of Fort Morgan opened fire on Farragut's fleet slightly more than an hour later. After more than half an hour of intense action, Farragut's lead ship, the USS *Tecumseh,* struck a torpedo (naval mine) and sank. At this point Farragut allegedly stated, "Damn the torpedoes—full speed ahead!"[14]

The Crater, Petersburg

The monumental explosion of the Petersburg mine ripped open the Confederate works and killed or wounded hundreds of Rebels in an instant. But in the attack that followed, Union soldiers became mired in the huge, smoking crater and were slaughtered in turn.

Fort Gaines, Mobile, Alabama

Heavy guns at Fort Gaines, along with those at nearby Forts Morgan and Powell, protected the entrance to Mobile Bay. In August 1864 the Federal navy under Rear Admiral David G. Farragut moved on Mobile. On August 4 Major General Gordon Granger's troops invested Fort Gaines, and Farragut's fleet would follow.

A photograph of Fort Morgan taken in 1864 shows damage to the south side of the fort.

National Archives and Records Administration

Fort Morgan, Mobile Bay

With Fort Gaines out of the action, Confederate cannoneers at Fort Morgan pounded Farragut's fleet but could not prevent its passage into Mobile Bay.

Farragut pressed through, pushed the *Tennessee* into surrender, and captured the spirits of northerners as another Union hero.

As Grant and Meade continued in their struggle against Lee at Petersburg and Sherman pushed more deeply into Georgia, a third operation began in the Union grand strategy of simultaneous movements. In August, Sheridan initiated a campaign to clear the Shenandoah Valley of Confederate troops and of military usefulness to the Confederacy. He faced Jubal Early, who had threatened Washing-

Fort Morgan

In the battle for Mobile Bay, Fort Morgan's gunners fired on Farragut's ships from casements such as this one.

ton the month before. On September 19 the two forces clashed at Winchester, where Sheridan won decisively and forced Early southward to Fisher's Hill. A letter written on this day underscores the uncertainty all parties had about the course of the war and the chances for politics to play a critical role. "The State election of Indiana occurs on the 11th of October," Abraham Lincoln wrote Sherman. "And the loss of it, to the friends of the Government would go far toward losing the whole Union cause. . . . Anything you can safely do to let her soldiers, or any part of them, go home and vote at the State election will be greatly in point."

Increasingly, the revivals in the southern armies led those who already had strong faith to look heavenward for help. "These are times calling for great sacrifices," wrote Confederate brigadier general Stephen Dodson Ramseur from the field near Staunton, Virginia, to his wife. "We must bear separation, hardship, and danger for the sake of our Country. We must dare and do in the Cause of liberty. We must never yield an inch, nor relax in any effort in the defence of our home or the establishment of our nationality. We will do our duty leaving the result to God." Twelve days later Ramseur was killed.

Southerners also celebrated their great general, who was becoming a legend

Fort Davidson, Pilot Knob, Missouri

Sterling Price's autumn 1864 raid into Missouri hit a roadblock in the form of Brigadier General Thomas Ewing Jr.'s Union garrison at Fort Davidson, near Pilot Knob (background). After a successful defense, Ewing evacuated the position and blew it up.

despite the military frustrations and the difficulty of life on the home front. "The Genl proposed that we should go [to church] to Mr. Gibson's," wrote Walter Taylor of his commanding officer, Robert E. Lee, on September 11. "It is quite trying to accompany the General to Church or any public place. Everybody crowds the way and stops on the pavements to have a look."[15]

In the western theater, Confederate major general Sterling Price launched a raid across Missouri that had little concrete strategic objective. The idea was to recover the state for the Confederacy, but the realism of such a goal had faded many months before. Nonetheless, Price captured Lexington on September 17–20 and proceeded to attack Fort Davidson near the distinctive mountain dubbed Pilot Knob. "Price arrived before Pilot Knob in the afternoon of September 26th," wrote Wiley Britton of the 6th Kansas Cavalry (U.S.A.), "and skirmished until night with detachments of Federal cavalry. . . . Price opened the attack on [Fort Davidson] at daylight on the 27th, and kept it up all day with great resolution."[16] The campaign was fruitless in the end, as Price retreated and then made a circuitous journey through Indian Territory to escape Federal forces.

As autumn began, the contest between Sheridan and Early in the Valley escalated. "To-morrow I will continue the destruction of wheat, forage, etc., down to Fisher's Hill," Sheridan wrote Grant from Woodstock on October 7. "When this is completed the Valley, from Winchester up to Staunton, ninety-two miles, will have little in it for man or beast."[17] He beat the Confederate force at Tom's Brook on October 9, but four days later Early made a show of force at Strasburg, compelling Sheridan to recall troops to Middletown. Returning from a conference in Washington, Sheridan heard the sounds of battle as he approached his army along the Valley Turnpike from Winchester to Cedar Creek on October 19. The

Belle Grove, Middletown, Virginia

In the fall of 1864 Grant dispatched Phil Sheridan to destroy the Shenandoah Valley's military usefulness once and for all. The decisive battle of Cedar Creek raged around Belle Grove, a house used by Sheridan as a headquarters.

Old State Capitol, Milledgeville, Georgia

As Sherman's "bummers" marched from Atlanta to Savannah, the Yankees inhabited the Capitol of Georgia in Milledgeville, held a mock session of the legislature, and "readmitted" the state into the Union. The building is now part of a military academy.

battle of Cedar Creek, fought in the fields near Middletown, seemed a rout of the Federals. Sheridan's presence, however, sparked his men into regrouping and counterattacking, and the resulting Union victory spelled the end of Confederate resistance in the Valley.

Throughout the fall, the growing legions of prisoners held in both northern and southern prisons suffered as never before. At its peak, Andersonville, in south central Georgia, became the third largest city in the Confederacy, with more than 33,000 residents. Such blots on the humanity of Americans on both sides of the war weighed heavily on the psychology of the home front. "Our quarters were so crowded that none of us had more space to himself than he actually occupied, usually a strip of the bare, hard floor, about six feet by two," wrote Abner Small, a Federal soldier formerly of the 16th Maine Infantry imprisoned in Danville, Virginia. "We lay in long rows, two rows of men with their heads to the side walls and two with their heads together along the center of the room." The scant rations given to prisoners led to horrific rates of death and disease. "A prisoner eating this [spare] diet will crave any kind of fresh meat," wrote Marcus Toney, a Confederate imprisoned at Elmira, New York. "Marching through the camp one day was a prisoner in a barrel shirt, with placard, 'I eat a dog'; another one bearing a barrel, with placard, 'Dog Eater.' . . . It appeared these prisoners had captured a lapdog owned by the baker who came into camp daily to bake bread."

As the situation on the battlefield grew ever more critical, the methods to which partisans resorted in hope of changing the course of the war were myriad. On November 25, for example, a band of Confederate agents attempted to burn New

York City. The conspirators attacked various hotels and well-known galleries (such as P. T. Barnum's) with incendiary devices, but the fires were controlled and the whole plan fizzled. "The bottles of Greek fire having been wrapped in paper were put in our coat pockets," wrote John W. Headley, one of the Confederate agents. "Each man took ten bottles. . . . I reached the Astor House . . . after lighting the gas jet I hung the bedclothes loosely on the headboard and piled the chairs, drawers of the bureau and washstand on the bed. Then stuffed some newspapers about among the mass and poured a bottle of turpentine over it all. . . . I opened a bottle carefully and quickly and spilled it on the pile of rubbish. It blazed up instantly and the whole bed seemed to be in flames, before I could get out."[18]

Despite such forays, the fears of Union loyalists were slowly dissipating, while those of the southern rebels were growing. Lincoln won the election handily. Although progress around the Petersburg trenches was slow, Sherman in mid-November embarked on a march from Atlanta to Savannah, destroying railroads

Winstead Hill, Franklin, Tennessee

John Bell Hood watched parts of the battle of Franklin from Winstead Hill. He cannot have enjoyed what he saw as his troops and officers suffered heavy casualties at the hands of the defending northerners.

and much else of military value to the Confederacy all along the way. He was virtually unopposed. "At three o'clock the watch-fires are burning dimly, and, but for the occasional neighing of horses, all is so silent that it is difficult to imagine that twenty thousand men are within a radius of a few miles," wrote George Ward Nichols, a staff officer of Sherman's, of the first days of the March to the Sea. "The ripple of the brook can be distinctly heard as it breaks over the pebbles, or winds petulantly about the gnarled roots. The wind sweeping gently through the tall pines overhead only serves to lull to deeper repose the slumbering soldier, who is in his tent dreaming of his far-off Northern home."[19]

Rather than opposing Sherman, Hood had believed that by turning northward and threatening lines of supply and communication in Tennessee (as well as endangering Union-held Nashville), he could draw Sherman away from the Deep South. He could not have been more wrong. Hood's Tennessee campaign began ingloriously for the Confederates and turned into full-fledged disaster. Marching northward from Florence, Alabama, Hood's army first encountered Union troops in force near Columbia, Tennessee, with Yankees north of the Duck River on November 27 and Confederates south of it. The Federal forces consisted of detachments from Major General George H. Thomas's force in Nashville. In the mid-afternoon of November 29, the battle of Spring Hill occurred, with piecemeal attacks mismanaged by Hood that ended in confusion. The Federal commander on the field, John Schofield, marched his troops along the Columbia Pike past bivouacked Confederates during the night, setting up the battle of Franklin the next day.

Hood attacked frontally at Franklin, recklessly exposing his troops to an entrenched position that inflicted murderous casualties on them. The flashpoint of

Fountain Branch Carter House, Franklin, Tennessee

The centerpiece of the battle line at Franklin was the Fountain Branch Carter House, today a beautifully preserved structure.

Carter Farm Office, Franklin, Tennessee

The ferocity of the battle at Franklin is evidenced by the Carter farm office building, whose clapboards bear the scars of Confederate volleys fired over the Union defenders. Rebuilt since the war, the building retains the original wood.

John McGavock House, Carnton, Franklin, Tennessee

Following the action at Franklin, the bodies of four slain Confederate generals lay on the porch at Carnton mansion south of the town.

the battle was the Fountain Branch Carter House and a nearby cotton gin, around which intense barrages of fire ignited throughout the late afternoon. Hood's frontal attacks cost the army men he could not afford to lose—more than 6,000 casualties, including six general officers dead or mortally wounded. Four of these generals were carried to a nearby mansion, the John McGavock House, Carnton, where they were laid out on the porch—Major General Patrick Cleburne, beloved as one of the greatest Confederate generals in the West, and Brigadier Generals John Adams, Otho F. Strahl, and Hiram B. Granbury. Two other Confederate brigadier generals, John C. Carter and States Rights Gist, died fighting at Franklin.

If Hood had badly damaged his Army of Tennessee at Franklin, he ruined it permanently two weeks later at Nashville. As Hood advanced from Franklin,

Federal officers in Nashville prepared to fight with every resource they had. "Every horse and mare that could be used was taken," wrote Major General James H. Wilson. "All street-car and livery stable horses, and private carriage- and saddle-horses, were seized. Even Andrew Johnson, the vice-president-elect, was forced to give up his pair. A circus then at Nashville lost everything except its ponies; even the old white trick horse was taken but it was alleged that the young and handsome equestrienne, who claimed him, succeeded in convincing my adjutant general that the horse was unfit for cavalry service."[20] On December 15 Hood's approach brought on an attack by Thomas over a broad front south of the city. The battle was a lopsided victory for the Union forces, and continued through part of the next day before the remains of Hood's army fled south.

Anything but obsessed by Hood, Sherman was at this moment approaching

Confederate Cemetery, Franklin, Tennessee

Due to pilfering of the dead, the rarity of identification tags, and a system of hasty burials and reburials, many thousands of Civil War soldiers lost not only their lives, but also their identities. Fifteen such anonymous Confederate soldiers lie together underneath this stone.

Savannah on his revolutionary March to the Sea. On December 20 he occupied the city with his 62,000 men scattered nearby, and sent Lincoln the message that he could offer a Christmas present, Savannah. A new legend was developing. "General Sherman is the most American looking man I ever saw," wrote John Chipman Gray, the Federal staff officer, on December 14, "tall and lank, not very

Fort Negley, Nashville, Tennessee

Hood's Army of Tennessee avoided complete destruction at Franklin, but that fate arrived on December 15 at the battle of Nashville. Fort Negley, one of the fortifications protecting the city that day, now amounts to a disheveled collection of stone slabs.

erect, with hair like a thatch, which he rubs up with his hands, a rusty beard trimmed close, a wrinkled face, sharp, prominent, red nose, small, bright eyes, coarse red hands; black felt hat slouched over the eyes."21 The final diamonds of the Confederacy were crumbling away, and time was running out rapidly now.

Green-Meldrim House, Savannah

On December 21 Sherman's troops reached Savannah essentially unopposed. "I beg to present you with a Christmas present," he wrote Lincoln, "the city of Savannah." Sherman established headquarters at the Green-Meldrim house, an elaborate brick and wrought-iron Italianate mansion.

"WE ARE ALL COMRADES AGAIN"

As a New Year began, the Confederacy was on its last legs. The siege operations around Petersburg ground on, sapping the remaining resources and supplies that could be brought to bear against the Union army. Hood's disastrous campaign in Tennessee had effectively eliminated the Army of Tennessee from further meaningful service in the war. A combined operation by the Federal army and navy was closing in on Wilmington, North Carolina, the last port open to supply the Confederacy. The Lincoln administration had won the autumn election decisively, pushing into the shadows the possibility of a peace movement in the North swaying the Yankees' actions. The Confederacy had lost many a hero in the past couple of years—Stonewall Jackson being only the most notable—and many southerners had lost faith in Jefferson Davis. They had now only a single general in the field on whom to place their great hopes, Robert E. Lee.

The growing sense of despair on the Confederate home front and in the ranks led to consideration of measures that would have been thought insane a year before. A number of officers and politicians mulled the hard thought of emancipating slaves as a source of new soldiers. Lee himself supported the idea, which gave it the kind of approval to be taken seriously in the Confederate Congress. In January 1865 the measure was debated without a conclusion. After all, the papers of the Confederacy's founders had clearly protected slavery and held it high as a great and necessary good. As Howell Cobb, an influential congressman from Georgia, wrote, "If slaves will make good soldiers, our whole theory of slavery is wrong."[1] Eventually the Congress did legislate the raising of black troops for field service in the Confederate army, but the measure came too late for any such

Stockade, Andersonville, Georgia

Of all the Civil War prison camps, Camp Sumter at Andersonville, in central Georgia, was the most notorious for its horrors. When it was evacuated at Sherman's approach, its mass trench graves held nearly 13,000 Union dead.

Andersonville prisoners receiving rations on August 17, 1864, as photographed by A. J. Riddle.

National Archives and Records Administration

troops to actually march outside Richmond. That it nearly became a reality' speaks of the desperation of the Confederate war effort.

By contrast, the psychology of the Union military was strongly unified. Soldiers and civilians alike began to sense the impending victory, and heroes had multiplied on the Federal side. Grant was locked in the struggle, along with Meade, against Lee in Virginia. But Sherman had emerged in 1864 as a leading figure who had accelerated the climax of the war. "I do think that in the several grand epochs of this war, my name will have a prominent part," wrote Sherman to his wife, Ellen, from Savannah on January 5. "And not least among them will be the determination I took at Atlanta to destroy that place, and march on this city, whilst Thomas, my lieutenant, should dispose of Hood."[2]

Having arrived at Savannah before Christmas, Sherman now trained his armies on the Carolinas. One of the duties of his invaders would be to liberate Union prisoners wherever they could be found. The prisoners at Andersonville had been moved before Sherman's approach, but Yankees were freed at Millen, Georgia, and other facilities. "It is dreadful. My heart aches for the poor wretches, Yankees though they are," wrote Eliza Andrews of the prisoners at Andersonville, "and I am afraid God will suffer some terrible retribution to fall upon us for letting such things happen."[3]

As Sherman contemplated turning northward, a major attack by the Federal army and navy was calculated to close Wilmington. The attack was aimed at Fort Fisher, which protected the entrance into the city. Major General Benjamin F. Butler had commanded an unsuccessful movement against Fort Fisher in December. Now Major General Alfred H. Terry was ordered to take the position. Terry's 8,000 men, constituting Terry's Provisional Corps, would be assisted by Rear Admiral David D. Porter's North Atlantic Blockading Squadron of sixty ships armed with a total of 627 guns.

Georgia Monument, Andersonville

Andersonville's Georgia Monument commemorates the suffering that occurred at this largest of Civil War prisons. At its peak during the summer of 1864, 32,899 men were incarcerated here, making it one of the largest cities in the Confederacy.

Fort Fisher Monument, Wilmington, North Carolina

As 1865 began, hopes for the Confederacy were dwindling. Wilmington, the last open southern seaport, was closed when on January 15 a Union army-navy operation assaulted Fort Fisher.

The flotilla arrived off the North Carolina coast on January 12. The Confederate district commander, Major General William H. C. Whiting, reinforced the garrison at Fort Fisher to nearly 2,000 troops, equipped with forty-seven artillery pieces. Just after midnight on January 13 the Federal ships opened fire on the fort, commanded by Colonel William Lamb, and during the following day troops landed to assault the position. Augustus Buell, a soldier in the 4th U.S. Artillery, described the bombardment of the thirteenth: "There would be two puffs of blue smoke about the size of a thunder cloud in June," he wrote, "and then I could see the big shell make a black streak through the air with a tail of white smoke behind it—and then would come over the water, not the quick bark of a field gun, but a slow, quivering, overpowering roar like an earthquake, and then, away among the Rebel traverses, there would be another huge ball of mingled smoke and flame as big as a meeting house."[4]

On January 15 a heavy naval bombardment commenced at close range, softening the position where the Federal attack would concentrate. Early in the afternoon a small force rushed forward and dug in close to the fort. Late in the day Federal soldiers stormed the fort in force, breaking into the parapets with axes and firing wildly at the defenders. Before nightfall the Yankees succeeded in capturing the position, along with nearly 2,000 soldiers, all the guns, and the mortally wounded Whiting. The last great Confederate port was closed.

On the Virginia front, operations were still frustratingly slow. Although Lee had prevented Grant from taking Petersburg (or destroying the Army of Northern Virginia), time was running out for the southern hero. "[Grant's] present force is so superior to ours, that if he is reinforced to any extent, I do not see how in our

Timothy O'Sullivan photographed the interior of Fort Fisher on January 1865 after its fall to Federal forces. Note the gun's exploded muzzle.

Library of Congress

present position he can be prevented from enveloping Richmond," Lee wrote Jefferson Davis on January 29. "Such a combination is his true policy & therefore I fear it is true."[5] At about this time, on January 23, the Confederate Congress reacted to the poor morale and lack of faith in Davis by creating the assignment of commander in chief of all Confederate armies, naming Robert E. Lee.

Lee's fears over Grant were about to come true. A peace conference held at Hampton Roads on February 3 led nowhere. Initiated by the aged Union politician Francis P. Blair Sr.—a member of Andrew Jackson's "Kitchen Cabinet"— the conference brought Confederate vice president Alexander H. Stephens, Assistant Secretary of War John A. Campbell, and Senator Robert M. T. Hunter together on board the USS *River Queen.* Meeting with the Confederate delegation was none other than President Lincoln, who told them that the Confederacy had virtually no room for bargaining in terms of surrender. The conference was inconclusive. Despite their desperate situation, many Confederates in positions of power failed to see the coming ruin. "Doubtless Lee could protract the war, and, by concentrating farther South, embarrass the enemy by compelling him to maintain a longer line of communication by land and by sea," wrote the war clerk John B. Jones on February 12. "Lee could have an army of 100,000 effective men for years."[6]

In fact Lee planned on a major attack at Petersburg that could stun Grant's army, enable Lee to hold Petersburg and Richmond with reduced numbers of men, and enable him to head south to unite with General Joe Johnston in the Carolinas, thereby gaining the opportunity to ruin Sherman's army. It was an unlikely plan that would never gain the opportunity for testing beyond the initial stage. "Something is about to happen," wrote Luther Rice Mills, a North Carolina

Confederate, on March 2. "I know not what. Nearly every one who will express an opinion says Gen'l Lee is about to evacuate Petersburg. . . . I would regret very much to give up the old place. The soiled and tattered Colors borne by our skeleton Regiments is sacred and dear to the hearts of every man." "People are almost in a state of desperation," wrote Josiah Gorgas on the same day. "Lee is about all we have & what public confidence is left rallies around him, and he it seems to me fights without much heart in the cause."[7]

But no attack yet came. In Washington, on March 4, Abraham Lincoln was inaugurated on the east portico of the Capitol, with Andrew Johnson of Tennessee becoming his vice president. Lincoln struggled to summarize the horrifying war that had lasted for nearly the entirety of his first term and had still not ended. Concluded Lincoln: "With malice toward none, with charity for all, with firmness in the right as God gives us to see the right, let us strive on to finish the work we are in, to bind up the nation's wounds, to care for him who shall have borne the battle and for his widow and his orphan, to do all which may achieve and cherish a just and lasting peace among ourselves and with all nations."[8]

Lee's attack finally came at Fort Stedman on the Petersburg front on the afternoon of March 25. An attempted breakthrough by troops led by Major General

Five Forks, Virginia

Grant's siege of Petersburg had exhausted the weary defenders, and when Sheridan struck Five Forks and cut their last rail supply route, the only remaining hope lay in flight. The final hunt was on.

John B. Gordon began well, but a counterattack by Major General John F. Hartranft stalled it. Now the situation for Lee deteriorated rapidly. Sheridan, who had defeated the scattered the remnants of Early's forces in the Valley, rejoined Grant. Movements by Major General Edward O. C. Ord on March 27–28 allowed Grant to send Sheridan and Warren westward to threaten the Southside Railroad, potentially severing Petersburg from the rest of the world. An explosive engagement along the White Oak Road on March 31 ended in Confederate failure, and the situation for Lee was crumbling. At Five Forks on April 1, Sheridan and Warren—despite confusion in orders and grogginess in executing them—struck and captured the force of 4,500 under Major General George E. Pickett. This blow eliminated the Southside Railroad as a supply route for Lee and forced the evacuation of Petersburg. Colonel William R. J. Pegram, a favorite artillery officer of Lee's, was mortally wounded at Five Forks. "Fire your canister low, men," he shouted, and then was hit: "Oh Gordon, I am mortally wounded, take me off the field."[9]

Struck heavily by Union artillery and a piercing set of attacks on the right flank, Lee's army was in a hopeless situation. Assaults on weak gaps in the Confederate lines continued through April 2, and Grant ordered assaults to continue on the following day. All Lee could do was to hope to escape under cover of darkness. He initiated a series of communications aimed at removing all war matériel from Richmond and sending it southward, where he would try to find Johnston. The withdrawal from Richmond began in good order, and plans were made to concentrate at Amelia Court House. The evacuation fires set to destroy supplies that would otherwise fall into Yankee hands burned from the Shockoe Warehouse district out of control, eventually destroying nearly one-third of the city. "I was wakened suddenly by four terrific explosions, one after the other, making the windows of my garret shake," wrote Constance Cary on April 4. "It was the blowing up, by Admiral Semmes, by order of the Secretary of the Navy, of our gunboats on the James, the signal for an all-day carnival of thundering noise and flames. Soon the fire spread, shells in the burning arsenals began to explode, and a smoke arose that shrouded the whole town, shutting out every vestige of blue sky and April sunshine. Flakes of fire fell around us, glass shattered, and chimneys fell."[10]

Far to the south, the prospects for Lee's meeting up with Joe Johnston were shrinking daily. Sherman moved out of Savannah and toward Columbia, South Carolina, where on February 17 an evacuation fire also destroyed much of that city. "I began to-day's record early in the evening, and while writing I noticed an unusual glare in the sky," wrote George Ward Nichols, of Sherman's staff, "and heard a sound of running to and fro in the streets, with the loud talk of servants that the horses must be removed to a safer place. Running out, I found, to my surprise and real sorrow, that the central part of the city, including the main business street, was in flames, while the wind, which had been blowing a hurricane all day, was driving the sparks and cinders in heavy masses over the eastern portion of the city."[11] On March 16 a portion of Johnston's command attempted to block Sherman at Averasboro but was beaten badly. Three days later, at Bentonville, Johnston's force hit Sherman squarely but again was defeated. Sherman planned to turn northward and meet up with Grant.

Following the fall of Richmond and Petersburg, Lee's army fled westward in what became the Appomattox campaign. The pursuit by Grant's army was quick and stunning. Lee concentrated at Amelia Court House on April 5, expecting to find supply trains; they never came. The following day, at Sayler's Creek, Federals cut off the Confederate rear guard, capturing more than 8,000 men, including six general officers. On the same day, former Virginia governor Henry A. Wise wrote Lee, "[There] has been no country, general, for a year or more." He added, "You are the country to these men. They have fought for you." The following day Lee reached Farmville, where his starving army received rations and a short rest, but nearby, at High Bridge, the Federal army struck again at his rear guard. On this day Lincoln, at City Point, wrote to Grant, "General Sheridan says 'If the thing is pressed I think that Lee will surrender.' Let the *thing* be pressed."[12]

Richmond-Lynchburg Stage Road, Appomattox Court House, Virginia

Lee's army fled westward, hoping to turn south and link with General Joe Johnston in the Carolinas. But Grant was not about to let his prey escape. When what was left of the Army of Northern Virginia approached Appomattox Court House, visible on this approach along the Richmond-Lynchburg Stage Road, they were surrounded.

The thing was pressed. By April 9 Lee was exhausted and surrounded at Appomattox Court House, with Sheridan's cavalry and the infantry of Major Generals Edward O. C. Ord and Charles Griffin blocking his forward movement, the mass of Grant and Meade's army behind him. It was over. Lee had no choice but to meet Grant and discuss surrender terms. The officers decided on the front parlor of the Wilmer McLean House in the village as the best available place. Deep irony attended the choice of location. Grant and Lee would meet in the home of the man who was driven from his house in Manassas, Virginia, after First Bull Run. Wilmer McLean could state that the war began in his backyard and ended in his front parlor.

Lieutenant Colonel Horace Porter, Grant's aide, encountered Lee before the meeting. "Lee . . . was fully six feet in height, and quite erect for one of his age, for he was Grant's senior by sixteen years," Porter wrote. "His hair and full beard were a silver-gray, and quite thick, except that the hair had become a little thin in front. He wore a new uniform of Confederate gray, buttoned up to the throat, and at his side he carried a long sword of exceedingly fine workmanship, the hilt studded with jewels. . . . His top-boots were comparatively new, and seemed to have on them some ornamental stitching of red silk. . . . A felt hat, which in color matched pretty closely that of the uniform, and a pair of long buckskin gauntlets lay beside him on the table."[13]

Wilmer McLean House, Appomattox Court House

Lee had no choice but to surrender. The event occurred on April 9 at the Wilmer McLean house. Although other Confederate armies still occupied the field, in truth the war was over.

The McLean House was photographed by Timothy O'Sullivan in April 1865 following the surrender.

Library of Congress

Grant's generous terms were accepted by Lee, and as the Federal commander returned to the field, he admonished cheering Federal soldiers who were celebrating the Rebels' defeat. "The war is over—the rebels are our countrymen again," said Grant. Lee bade farewell to his beloved army and made plans to returned to Richmond. He was now a paroled prisoner, like his soldiers. "With an increasing admiration of your constancy and devotion to your country," he wrote for them, "and a grateful remembrance of your kind and generous consideration of myself, I bid you an affectionate farewell."

"How can I write it?" wondered North Carolina diarist Catherine Edmondston. "How find words to tell what has befallen us? *Gen Lee has surrendered!* . . . We stand appalled at our disaster! . . . [That] Lee, Lee upon whom hung the hopes of the whole country, should be a prisoner seems almost too dreadful to be realized!"[14]

Wilmer McLean House

Lee's surrender to Grant took place in this room, the front parlor of the McLean house.

Surrender Triangle, Appomattox Court House

On April 12, soldiers of the Army of Northern Virginia stacked their arms and furled their battle flags for the last time on the Surrender Triangle.

Despite the fact that Lee's army was just one of several left in the field, its surrender signaled an obvious end to the conflict. Just five days later a symbolic ending seemed to come with the raising of Old Glory over Fort Sumter, starting place of the war. "The ceremony began with a short prayer by the old army chaplain who had prayed when the flag was hoisted over Fort Sumter on December 27, 1860," wrote Mary Cadwalader Jones, who witnessed the event. "Next a Brooklyn clergyman read parts of several Psalms. . . . Then Sergeant Hart, who had held up the flag when its staff was shot through in the first attack, came forward quietly and drew the selfsame flag out of an ordinary leather mail bag. We all held our breath for a second, and then we gave a queer cry, between a cheer and a yell."[15]

And then, just as the celebrations were gaining steam across the North, the unthinkable happened. On April 14 Abraham Lincoln was assassinated by the actor John Wilkes Booth at Ford's Theatre in Washington. Carried to a house across the street, Lincoln died at 7:22 the next morning. "The giant sufferer lay extended diagonally across the bed, which was not long enough for him," wrote Navy Secretary Gideon Welles. "He had been stripped of his clothes. His large arms, which were occasionally exposed, were of a size which one would scarce have expected from his spare appearance. His slow, full respiration lifted the clothes with each breath that he took. His features were calm and striking."[16]

Lincoln's death marked the end of any possibility of a smooth, peaceful reconciliation with the former states in rebellion. Now the radical Republicans would rise to influence and help to administer a stern era of Reconstruction that would follow. But the heartaches of Reconstruction would spread over the coming years: in mid-April 1865, the war wasn't really over yet. On April 17, at Durham Sta-

Lafayette Meeks Grave, Appomattox Court House

The war had cost more than 620,000 lives. Among the Confederate dead was Lafayette Meeks, a Confederate soldier from Appomattox Court House who died just five days before the surrender and lies buried a short walk from the McLean house.

Petersen House, Washington, D.C.

Lincoln died in this small room in the Petersen house, across 10th Street from Ford's Theatre.

The presidential box photographed days after the assassination.

Library of Congress

"President's Box," Ford's Theatre, Washington, D.C.

The man who steered the course of the war would not live to see its end. On April 14 Abraham and Mary Todd Lincoln watched Our American Cousin *at Ford's Theatre in Washington. Shortly after 10 P.M. John Wilkes Booth shot the president, mortally wounding him. Booth escaped into Virginia but he, too, would die before the month's end.*

tion, North Carolina, Sherman forced Joe Johnston's army into an armistice. Nine days later, after managing the terms and negotiations with the intervention of U. S. Grant and the War Department, Sherman received Johnston's surrender at Bennett Place, a nearby farm. Johnston's capitulation was the first of the series of smaller surrenders that followed Lee's. On May 4 Lieutenant General Richard Taylor, son of the twelfth U.S. president, surrendered his force at Citronville, Alabama. Six days later, at Irwinville, Georgia, Federal cavalry caught up with the flight of the official party from Richmond, which included Jefferson Davis and his family. An overcoat hastily thrown over Davis's form as he attempted escape incited nasty press in the North about his supposed attempt to impersonate a woman. Also on March 10, Major General Samuel Jones surrendered his force at

Haywood House, Raleigh, North Carolina

On April 24 Grant traveled to Raleigh to meet with Sherman, whose proposed terms of surrender for General Joe Johnston had met disapproval in Washington. The two commanders met in the Haywood House, where they ironed out a solution.

Bennett Place, Durham Station, North Carolina

Johnston surrendered to Sherman on April 26 at Bennett Place near Durham Station. The second army of the Confederacy now lost its arms, and the end of the war was solidified.

**Fort Smith National Cemetery,
Fort Smith, Arkansas**

After the war the business of collecting the dead of both armies continued apace, and thousands of slain soldiers were sent home or buried in newly established national cemeteries.

Tallahassee, Florida. The next day Colonel M. Jeff Thompson, the famed partisan ranger, gave up his men at Chalk Bluff, Arkansas.

On May 12–13, at Palmito Ranch, Texas (near Brownsville), the last engagement of the Civil War was fought. The action, involving a few hundred soldiers on each side, ironically resulted in a decisive Confederate victory. But it was the last gasp of a dead military effort. No more actions of significance took place, and way out west, in the Trans-Mississippi, General Edmund Kirby Smith finally surrendered on June 2, at Galveston, Texas. The Confederacy was gone. "And now, with my latest writing and utterance, and with what will be near to my latest breath, I here repeat, and would willingly proclaim, my unmitigated hatred to Yankee rule," wrote Edmund Ruffin, the fiery South Carolina secessionist, on June 18, "to all political, social, and business connection with the Yankees, and to the perfidious, malignant, and vile Yankee race."[17] He then killed himself.

In Washington, despite the loss of their beloved commander, northerners celebrated the conclusion of the war by marching their two victorious armies through the streets of the capital. On May 23, as President Johnson, U. S. Grant, and numerous other officials and military officers watched, Meade's Army of the Potomac, some 80,000 strong, marched through the city and down Pennsylvania Avenue. The next day, Sherman's Army of Georgia and Army of the Tennessee, together some 65,000 strong, marched the same route. The contrast between the well-dressed easterners and the dirty, exhausted westerners (who had just undertaken a 2,000-mile march) was striking, but all spectators cheered with great enthusiasm. Bunting and other decor for the fallen president adorned the whole of the city.

**Jefferson Davis Home, Beauvoir,
Biloxi, Mississippi**

Refusing to accept the outcome of the conflict, Jefferson Davis fled south. Captured near Irwinville, Georgia, he spent two years as a prisoner at Fort Monroe, Virginia. In 1877 Davis retired to this house, Beauvoir, and lived the final twelve years of his life.

Ulysses S. Grant Home, Galena, Illinois

Postwar life for Ulysses S. Grant included two terms in the White House beginning in 1868, and then a struggle to pen his memoirs as he was dying from throat cancer. Immediately after the war, a hero's welcome in Galena included the gift of this house.

It had seemed like eternal night. The time from the bombardment of Sumter to the surrender of Kirby Smith's troops in Galveston comprised 1,512 days of darkness. More than three million enlistments for service had been recorded, and more than 620,000 men had lost their lives—not counting the lingering effects of wounds that would bring thousands of others an early death in the years to follow. For most of the Civil War soldiers—who were considerably younger and thinner than those in the movies—the war promised to be a thrilling adventure and turned out to be a sentence of drudgery and endless boredom punctuated by short, violent episodes of terror. Yet for most it was the greatest time of their lives, and they could not shake the memories and the camaraderie after they returned home to the many reuniting states of the reconciled nation.

The "erring sisters" were readmitted into the Union, one by one. In 1866 Tennessee came back. In 1868 came Florida, Arkansas, North Carolina, Louisiana, South Carolina, and Alabama. In 1870 came Virginia, Mississippi, Texas, and finally, Georgia. In a legal sense, at least, the country was again unified.

As the shock of endless blood, the booming of the cannon and the crackle of musketry, and the horrors of the photographs of Brady, Gardner, and O'Sullivan began to wear slightly into the background, Americans struggled to make sense of it all. "Future years will never know the seething hell and the black infernal background of countless minor scenes and interiors of the Secession War," wrote Walt Whitman in 1875. "In the mushy influences of current times the fervid atmosphere and typical events of those years are in danger of being totally forgotten."[18] The veterans took refuge in societal organizations that allowed them to relive the war, continue their soldierly attitudes, and put civilian life in the new America into perspective. The largest such organization, the Grand Army of the

P. G. T. Beauregard Tomb, Metairie Cemetery, New Orleans

Some former generals lived in luxury after the war. Beauregard, hero of Sumter, First Bull Run, and Drewry's Bluff, became a railroad president and supervisor of the Louisiana Lottery. He died in 1893 after being worshiped widely in the South.

War Correspondent's Arch, Crampton's Gap, South Mountain, Maryland

Many survivors gathered frequently to recall the war's great events. George Alfred Townsend, correspondent for the New York Herald, *built an estate on South Mountain where veterans from both armies met. His memorial arch pays tribute to the "bohemian brigade" that brought the war's news to the home front.*

Republic (for Union veterans), gained a peak membership of 409,489 in 1890 and actively supported Republican political issues. The Military Order of the Loyal Legion of the United States, a similar organization for officers only, published numerous important papers and actively supported the movement to create parks that would preserve the most significant battle areas of the war. On the Confeder-

Magnolia Cemetery, Charleston, South Carolina

Slowly, as the war began to fade, burial grounds like Charleston's Magnolia Cemetery were frequented by city residents. In 1866, at Blandford Cemetery in Petersburg, Mary Logan—wife of Senator and former Union general John A. Logan—noted young girls decorating graves. The resulting legislation created Decoration Day, which became Memorial Day.

ate side, the United Confederate Veterans had a maximum membership of about 80,000 in 1903.

And in the intervening decades, numerous participants (and journalists) continued to fight the war on paper. In the early years after the war, indeed, the South seemed to win the battles as they were recapitulated—and why not the whole war? Certain writers, like Ambrose Bierce, who had been a Federal officer, worried over the accuracy of much of what appeared in print, and lamented the fallen soldiers who never saw the country reunited again—who never knew how things would be. "They were the honest and courageous foemen, having little in common with the political madmen who persuaded them to their doom and the literary bearers of false witness in the aftertime," Bierce wrote in 1903. "They did not live through the period of honorable strife into the period of vilification—did not pass from the iron age to the brazen—from the era of the sword to that of the tongue and the pen."[19]

As the years rolled on, the aging veterans answered their last roll call with increasing rapidity. In the early twentieth century, veterans—although many were

General's Row, Greenwood Cemetery, Jackson, Mississippi

In years after the war survivors and their children traveled to numerous graveyards to visit the war's heroes. In Jackson, Mississippi, they found four Confederate brigadier generals, William Barksdale (who died at Gettysburg), Daniel W. Adams (1872), James A. Smith (1901), and Samuel W. Ferguson (1917).

Confederate Soldiers' Pyramid, Hollywood Cemetery, Richmond, Virginia

In the late 1880s ladies of the Hollywood Memorial Association raised funds to erect a granite pyramid 45 feet square and 90 feet high in Richmond's Hollywood Cemetery. The monument honors the 12,000 Confederate soldiers buried on the grounds.

now in old soldiers' homes—were still relatively common. Some even marched in infrequent parades, attended reunions (such as the fiftieth-anniversary celebration at Gettysburg in 1913), and watched the modern world emerge from what seemed an ancient past. The first battlefield parks—Chickamauga and Chattanooga, Gettysburg, Antietam, Shiloh, and Vicksburg—were initiated in the 1890s, and other historic sites came to be preserved at least in part. A few important players in the story of the Civil War remained, such as Nelson Miles (who lived until 1925), John R. Brooke (1926), and the last surviving substantive general, Adelbert Ames (1933). Increasingly, the war was now being recalled not by living flesh but in stone.

**Andersonville National Cemetery,
Andersonville, Georgia**

Dorrance Atwater and others worked tirelessly to catalog and identify as many of the Andersonville victims as they could.

At the dedication of the Lincoln Memorial in Washington in 1922, Robert Todd Lincoln participated in the ceremonies honoring his father. In the same year, the heroic equestrian statue of Ulysses S. Grant was unveiled on the west front of the Capitol. The Civil War monument with the longest history of construction is surely Stone Mountain, the granite dome east of Atlanta, on which Gutzon Borglum and a team of sculptors initiated the elaborate bas-relief sculpture of the three foremost heroes of the Confederacy, Robert E. Lee, Jefferson Davis, and Stonewall Jackson. Begun in 1916, the work was not finished until 1972. During this lengthy period, the last verifiable Union combat soldier of the war died, Albert Woolson of Minnesota, in 1956. Records for aged Confederate survivors who lasted longer are sketchy. Recorded as the last alleged Confederate soldier, Walter W. Williams died in 1959.

On the eve of the Civil War Centennial, the last survivors were dead. Now, another thirty-five years hence, a new generation of Americans has seemingly dis-

Abraham Lincoln Tomb, Oak Ridge Cemetery, Springfield, Illinois

As time passed, cities took on a mystique associated with the great leaders who lived in them. Public donations made possible an elaborate tomb for Abraham Lincoln in Springfield, finished in 1874.

Lee Recumbent Statue, Washington and Lee University, Lexington, Virginia

In 1883 a huge crowd assembled in Lexington to witness the unveiling of the Robert E. Lee Recumbent Statue, by Edward V. Valentine. Placed over Lee's crypt, the statue represents the general sleeping on the battlefield.

Robert E. Lee Monument, Richmond, Virginia

By 1890 Richmond's Monument Avenue featured the most elaborate equestrian monument of Robert E. Lee ever produced, an effort by Jean Antoine Mercié.

covered the fascination with the nation's gravest and most electrifying period. One can still walk along a path at Cheatham Hill near Kennesaw Mountain and see the black hull of a "witness tree," a tree known to have stood during Sherman's battle, but such living witnesses are rare and mute. We are now consigned

Stonewall Jackson Grave, Stonewall Jackson Memorial Cemetery, Lexington, Virginia

In Lexington, a heroic bronze statue of Stonewall Jackson stands in the center of the cemetery named for him. He was removed from the original burial position, located nearby in the Jackson family plot.

William T. Sherman Grave, Calvary Cemetery, St. Louis, Missouri

Few important commanders of the war lasted until the twentieth century. William T. Sherman died in 1891 and was buried in a stately but rather modest plot in St. Louis.

Ulysses S. Grant Monument, Washington, D.C.

The most renowned monument to a Civil War general may be that of Ulysses S. Grant, positioned in front of the west portico of the U.S. Capitol. Executed by Henry M. Shrady, it was dedicated in 1922.

Stone Mountain, Georgia

In 1916 Gutzon Borglum initiated the carving of Stone Mountain, east of Atlanta, which would feature equestrian bas-relief figures of Jefferson Davis, Robert E. Lee, and Stonewall Jackson. The mammoth project was not finished until 1972.

Witness Tree, Cheatham Hill, Kennesaw Mountain, Georgia

Few living witnesses to Civil War battles remain. This tree near a visitor's path on Cheatham Hill near Kennesaw Mountain stood during Sherman's campaign of 1864.

Lincoln Memorial, Washington, D.C. *(right)*

Perhaps the most visited Civil War monument is the Lincoln Memorial. Dedicated in 1922 and containing the famous sculpture by Daniel Chester French, the memorial features the phrase, "In this temple as in the hearts of the American people for whom he saved the Union, the memory of Abraham Lincoln is enshrined forever."

to understanding this most dramatic of national periods in the pages of books, connecting emotionally with the issues in motion pictures such as *Glory* and *Gettysburg,* and feeling a sense of closeness to the past by visiting the battlefields and historic sites themselves. There, more than anywhere else, we may come to appreciate what the Civil War really accomplished. In the words attributed to poet Carl Sandburg, it transformed the phrase "these United States are" into "this United States is."

The Sunken Road, Sharpsburg, Maryland

The sun having set long ago on the war's last living memories, the reminders now left behind are all fashioned from stone, as with this monument at Antietam's Sunken Road.

NOTES

STORM CLOUDS ON THE HORIZON

1. Carl Sandburg, *Abraham Lincoln: The War Years* (New York: Harcourt, Brace, 1939), I, 1–3.

2. Abraham Lincoln, *The Collected Works of Abraham Lincoln,* ed. Roy P. Basler (New Brunswick, N.J.: Rutgers University Press, 1953–1955), IV, 271; Wilder Dwight, *The Life and Letters of Wilder Dwight, Lieut.-Col. Second Mass. Inf. Vols.* (Boston: Ticknor and Fields, 1868), 33–34.

3. Lincoln, *Collected Works,* II, 461–69.

4. Stephen Oates, *To Purge This Land with Blood: A Biography of John Brown* (New York: Harper and Row, 1970), 351.

5. Lincoln, *Collected Works,* IV, 151.

6. Frank Moore, ed., *The Rebellion Record: A Diary of American Events, with Documents, Narratives, Illustrative Incidents, Poetry, etc.* (New York: G. P. Putnam's Sons, 1861–1863 and D. Van Nostrand, 1864–1868; supplemental vol., G. P. Putnam's Sons and Henry Holt, 1864), I, 2; William H. Pease and Jane H. Pease, *James Louis Petigru: Southern Conservative, Southern Dissenter* (Athens: University of Georgia Press, 1995), 156.

7. Mary Boykin Chesnut, *Mary Chesnut's Civil War,* ed. C. Vann Woodward (New Haven: Yale University Press, 1981), 25.

8. Thomas Cooper DeLeon, *Four Years in Rebel Capitals: An Inside View of Life in the Southern Confederacy, from Birth to Death, from Original Notes, Collated in the Years 1861 to 1865* (Mobile, Ala.: Gossip Printing, 1890), 23–27; Jefferson Finis Davis, *The Papers of Jefferson Davis,* ed. Haskell M. Monroe Jr., James T. McIntosh, Lynda Lasswell Crist, Mary Seaton Dix, Richard E. Beringer, and Kenneth H. Williams, 9 vols. to date (Baton Rouge: Louisiana State University Press, 1971–1997), VII, 46–51.

9. Chesnut, *Mary Chesnut's Civil War,* 46.

10. Louis P. Masur, ed., *The Real War Will Never Get in the Books: Selections from Writers during the Civil War* (New York: Oxford University Press, 1993), 21.

11. Lyon G. Tyler, ed., *The Letters and Times of the Tylers* (New York: Da Capo Press, 1970), II, 641.

12. Robert E. Lee, *The Wartime Papers of R. E. Lee,* ed. Clifford Dowdey and Louis H. Manarin (Boston: Little, Brown, 1961), 9–10; *ibid,* 8.

13. Alexander K. McClure, ed., *The Annals of the War Written by Leading Participants North and South: Originally Published in the* Philadelphia Weekly Times (Philadelphia: Times Publishing, 1879), 775; *Chicago Tribune,* April 29, 1861, in *Rebellion Record,* ed. Moore, I, 147.

14. Michael Fitch, *Echoes of the Civil War As I Hear Them* (New York: R. F. Fenno, 1905), 20; Noah Brooks, *Washington in Lincoln's Time* (New York: Century, 1895), 15.

15. Nathaniel Hawthorne, from "Chiefly about War Matters," *Atlantic Monthly* (July 1862), 43–61, in *The Real War Will Never Get in the Books,* ed. Masur, 171; John B. Jones, *A Rebel War Clerk's Diary at the Confederate States Capital* (Philadelphia: J. B. Lippincott, 1866), I, 36.

16. Carlton McCarthy, *Detailed Minutiae of Soldier Life in the Army of Northern Virginia, 1861–1865* (Richmond: C. McCarthy, 1882), 16; Theodore Winthrop, *Life in the Open Air, and Other Papers* (Boston: Ticknor and Fields, 1863), 271.

17. Mary Anna Jackson, *Life and Letters of General Thomas J. Jackson (Stonewall Jackson)* (New York: Harper and Bros., 1892), 179.

18. Charles Minor Blackford, *Memoirs of Life in and out of the Army in Virginia during the War between the States,* ed. Susan Leigh Colston Blackford (Lynchburg, Va.: J. P. Bell, 1894–1896), 36.

19. William Howard Russell, *My Diary North and South* (New York: Harper and Bros., 1954), 223–24; Allen Thorndike Rice, ed., "A Page of Political Correspondence: Unpublished Letters of Mr. Stanton to Mr. Buchanan," *North American Review* 129 (1879): 482; Jackson, *Life and Letters of General Thomas J. Jackson,* 177.

20. George B. McClellan, *The Civil War Papers of George B. McClellan: Selected Correspondence, 1860–1865,* ed. Stephen W. Sears (New York: Ticknor and Fields, 1989), 70.

21. Charles E. Davis Jr., *Three Years in the Army: The Story of the Thirteenth Massachusetts Volunteers, from July 16, 1861, to August 1, 1864* (Boston: Estes and Lauriat, 1894), 3–99; John D. Billings, *Hardtack and Coffee; or, the Unwritten Story of Army Life, including Chapters on Enlisting, Life in Tents and Log Huts, Jonahs and Beats, Offences and Punishments, Raw Recruits, Foraging, Corps and Corps Badges, the Wagon Trains, the Army Mule, the Engineer Corps, etc.* (Boston: George M. Smith, 1887), 110; William Thompson Lusk, *War Letters of William Thompson Lusk, Captain, Assistant Adjutant-General United States Volunteers, 1861–1863* (New York: published by the author, 1911), 72–76.

22. Samuel Phillips Day, *Down South; or, An Englishman's Experience at the Seat of the American War* (London: Hurst and Blackett, 1862), II, 186.

23. Stephen W. Sears, *George B. McClellan: The Young Napoleon* (New York: Ticknor and Fields, 1988), 119.

24. Randolph Abbott Shotwell, "Three Years in Battle," in *The Papers of Randolph Abbott Shotwell,* ed. J. G. Roulhac Hamilton (Raleigh, N.C.: North Carolina Historical Commission, 1936), I, 113–19; Charles F. Johnson, *The Long Roll, being a Journal of the*

Civil War, as set down during the Years 1861–1863 (East Aurora, N.Y.: Roycrofters, 1911), 63–64.

25. Eugene Lawrence, "Grant on the Battle-Field," *Harper's New Monthly* 39 (1869): 212.

A BITTER YEAR OF HARD-FOUGHT WAR

1. James A. Connolly, "Major Connolly's Letters to His Wife, 1862–1865," *Transactions of the Illinois State Historical Society for the Year 1928* [Publications of the Illinois State Historical Library, No. 35] (Springfield, Ill.: Illinois State Historical Library, 1928), 220–24.

2. Ulysses S. Grant, *The Papers of Ulysses S. Grant,* ed. John Y. Simon (Carbondale, Ill.: Southern Illinois University Press, 1967–1995), IV, 218.

3. William Watson, *Life in the Confederate Army, being the Observations and Experiences of an Alien in the South during the American Civil War* (London: Chapman and Hall, 1887), 320–39.

4. Gershom J. Van Brunt, "Report of Captain Van Brunt," to Gideon Welles, 10 March 1862, *Official Records of the Union and Confederate Navies* [hereinafter cited as *ORN*] (Washington, D.C.: U.S. Government Printing Office, 1894–1927), I:VII, 11.

5. Fenwick Y. Hedley, *Marching through Georgia: Pen Pictures of Every-Day Life in General Sherman's Army, from the Beginning of the Atlanta Campaign until the Close of the War* (Chicago: R. R. Donnelly and Sons, 1885), 46.

6. Leander Stillwell, *The Story of a Common Soldier of Army Life in the Civil War, 1861–1865* (Kansas City, Mo.: Franklin Hudson, 1920), 42–52.

7. Henry M. Stanley, *The Autobiography of Sir Henry Morton Stanley,* ed. Dorothy Stanley (New York: Houghton Mifflin, 1909), 187–200.

8. Garnet Wolseley, "A Month's Visit to Confederate Headquarters," *Blackwood's Edinburgh Magazine* 93 (January–June 1863): 21; Jackson, *Life and Letters of General Thomas J. Jackson,* 249.

9. William Pittenger, "The Locomotive Chase in Georgia," *Century Magazine* 14 (1886): 141.

10. Julia LeGrand, *The Journal of Julia LeGrand: New Orleans, 1862–1863,* ed. Kate Mason Rowland and Mrs. Morris L. Croxall (Richmond: Everett Waddey, 1911), 39–43; Masur, ed., *The Real War Will Never Get in the Books,* 176.

11. McClellan, *Civil War Papers of George B. McClellan,* 257.

12. Jones, *Rebel War Clerk's Diary,* I, 128.

13. Evander M. Law, "The Fight for Richmond," *Southern Bivouac* 2 (April 1867), 649.

14. Alexander Hunter, *Johnny Reb and Billy Yank* (New York: Neale, 1905), 155–58.

15. Robert Stiles, *Four Years under Marse Robert* (New York: Neale, 1903), 97–99.

16. Oliver W. Norton, *Army Letters, 1861–1865, being Extracts from Private Letters to Relatives and Friends from a Soldier in the Field during the Late Civil War, with an Appendix Containing Copies of Some Official Documents, Papers, and Addresses of a Later Date* (Chicago: O. L. Deming, 1903), 92; Thomas L. Livermore, *Days and Events, 1860–1866* (Boston: Houghton Mifflin, 1920), 86–90.

17. Robert L. Dabney, *Life and Campaigns of Lieut.-Gen. Thomas J. Jackson (Stonewall Jackson)* (London: James Nisbet, 1864–1866), 516–18; Herman Haupt, *Reminiscences of General Herman Haupt: Giving Hitherto Unpublished Official Orders, Personal Narratives of Important Military Operations, and Interviews with President Lincoln, Secretary Stanton, General-in-Chief Halleck, and with Generals McDowell, McClellan, Meade, Hancock, Burnside, and Others in Command of the Armies in the Field, and His Impressions of These Men* (Milwaukee: Wright and Joys, 1901), 78, 80, 82.

18. Edward McCrady Jr., "Gregg's Brigade in the Second Battle of Manassas," *Southern Historical Society Papers* 13 (1885): 32.

19. Charles F. Walcott, "The Battle of Chantilly," *Papers of the Military Historical Society of Massachusetts* 2 (1895; The Virginia Campaign of 1862 under General Pope), 145.

20. Joseph Hooker, report on the battle of Antietam, in *The War of the Rebellion: A Compilation of the Official Records of the Union and Confederate Armies* [hereinafter cited as *OR*] (Washington, D.C.: U.S. Government Printing Office, 1880–1901), XIX:I, 218.

21. John B. Gordon, *Reminiscences of the Civil War* (New York: Charles Scribner's Sons, 1903), 90.

22. David I. Thompson, "With Burnside at Antietam," *Battles and Leaders of the Civil War, Being for the Most Part Contributions by Union and Confederate Officers: Based upon "The Century" War Series,* ed. Robert Underwood Johnson and Clarence Clough Buel (New York: Century, 1887–1888), II, 661–62; Frank Holsinger, "How Does One Feel under Fire?" *Papers of the Military Order of the Loyal Legion of the United States, 1887–1915* 15 (*War Talks in Kansas,* Kansas City, Mo.: Franklin Hudson, 1906): 301; Robert E. Lee Jr., *Recollections and Letters of General Robert E. Lee* (New York: Doubleday, Page, 1904), 78.

23. Lincoln, *Collected Works,* V, 433–36.

24. Abner Small, *The Road to Richmond: The Civil War Memoirs of Major Abner R. Small of the Sixteenth Maine Volunteers, together with the Diary which he kept when he was a Prisoner of War,* ed. Harold R. Small (Berkeley: University of California Press, 1939), 196–97.

25. Oscar L. Jackson, *The Colonel's Diary: Journals Kept before and during the Civil War, by the Late Colonel Oscar L. Jackson of New Castle, Pennsylvania, Sometime Commander of the 63d Regiment O.V.I.* (Sharon, Pa.: privately published, 1922), 70–76.

26. Lincoln, *Collected Works,* V, 518–37.

27. William N. Pendleton, *Southern Magazine* 15 (1874): 620; W. C. King and W. P. Derby, eds., *Camp-Fire Sketches and Battle-Field Echoes of '61–5* (Springfield, Mass.: W. C. King, 1887), 127–30.

28. David W. Blight, *Frederick Douglass' Civil War: Keeping Faith in Jubilee* (Baton Rouge: Louisiana State University Press, 1989), 115.

ZENITH OF THE CONFEDERACY

1. David Hunter Strother, *A Virginia Yankee in the Civil War: The Diaries of David Hunter Strother,* ed. Cecil D. Eby (Chapel Hill, N.C.: University of North Carolina Press, 1961), 112.

2. Lincoln, *Collected Works,* VI, 78–79.

3. John Esten Cooke, *Wearing of the Gray, being Personal Portraits, Scenes, and Adventures of the War* (Baltimore: E. B. Treat, 1867), 37.

4. Livermore, *Days and Events,* 203.

5. Johann August Heinrich Heros von Borcke, *Memoirs of the Confederate War for Independence* (Edinburgh: W. Blackwood and Sons, 1866), II, 241.

6. James Power Smith, "Stonewall Jackson's Last Battle," *Battles and Leaders,* ed. Johnson and Buel, III, 211.

7. Darius N. Couch, "The Chancellorsville Campaign," ibid., III, 169.

8. Oliver Otis Howard, "The Eleventh Corps at Chancellorsville," ibid., III, 202.

9. Benjamin H. Grierson, letter to John A. Rawlins, Baton Rouge, Louisiana, May 5, 1863, in *OR,* XXIV:I, 522.

10. William Tecumseh Sherman, *Home Letters of General Sherman,* ed. M. A. DeWolfe Howe (New York: Charles Scribner's Sons, 1909), 268–69.

11. Anonymous, Vicksburg, Miss., March 20, 1863, from "A Woman's Diary of the Siege of Vicksburg; Under Fire from the Gunboats," ed. George Washington Cable, *Century Illustrated* 8 (1885): 767.

12. Andrew Hickenlooper, "The Vicksburg Mine," *Battles and Leaders,* ed. Johnson and Buel, III, 542.

13. Joseph G. Rosengarten, "General Reynolds' Last Battle," *Annals of the War,* ed. McClure, 63.

14. John Bell Hood to James Longstreet, June 28, 1875, in *Southern Historical Society Papers* (Richmond: Southern Historical Society, 1877), IV, 150.

15. Theodore Gerrish, *Army Life: A Private's Reminiscences of the Civil War* (Portland, Maine: Hoyt, Fogg, and Donham, 1882), 111.

16. Evander M. Law, "The Struggle for Round Top," *Battles and Leaders,* ed. Johnson and Buel, III, 327.

17. James Longstreet, *From Manassas to Appomattox: Memoirs of the Civil War in America* (Philadelphia: J. B. Lippincott, 1896), 392.

18. Edmund Rice, "Repelling Lee's Last Blow at Gettysburg," *Battles and Leaders,* ed. Johnson and Buel, III, 389–90; Frank Aretas Haskell, "Haskell of Gettysburg: His Life and Civil War Papers," ed. Frank L. Byrne and Andrew T. Weaver (Madison, Wisc.: State Historical Society of Wisconsin, 1970), 170.

19. Ulysses S. Grant, "The Vicksburg Campaign," *Battles and Leaders,* ed. Johnson and Buel, III, 536

20. Lincoln, *Collected Works,* VI, 409.

21. *New York Tribune,* account composed at Morris Island, S.C., July 19, 1863, in *Rebellion Record,* ed. Moore, VII, 211–14.

22. James R. Carnahan, "Personal Recollections of Chickamauga," in *Sketches of War History, 1861–1865; Papers Read before the Ohio Commandery of the Military Order of the Loyal Legion of the United States, 1883–1886* (Cincinnati: Robert Clarke, 1888), I, 410–17; William Miller Owen, *In Camp and Battle with the Washington Artillery of New Orleans: A Narrative of Events during the Late Civil War from Bull Run to Appomattox and Spanish Fort* (Boston: Ticknor and Fields, 1885), 278–84.

23. Gates P. Thruston, "The Crisis at Chickamauga," *Battles and Leaders,* ed. Johnson and Buel, III, 664.

24. Kate Cumming, *Gleanings from Southland: Sketches of Life and Manners of the People of the South before, during, and after the War of Secession* (Birmingham, Ala.: Roberts, 1895), 135–44.

25. Joseph B. Polley, *A Soldier's Letters to Charming Nellie* (New York: Neale, 1908), 142–48.

26. Samuel H. M. Byers, "Sherman's Attack at the Tunnel," *Battles and Leaders,* ed. Johnson and Buel, III, 713.

27. James A. Connolly, "Major Connolly's Letters to His Wife, 1862–1865," *Transactions of the Illinois State Historical Society for the Year 1928* 35 (1928): 298.

28. Braxton Bragg to Jefferson Davis, Dec. 1, 1863, in *OR,* LII:II, 745.

29. Edward Porter Alexander, "Longstreet at Knoxville," *Battles and Leaders,* ed. Johnson and Buel, III, 749; Orlando M. Poe, "The Defense of Knoxville," ibid., III, 743.

30. Lincoln, *Collected Works,* VII, 17–22.

THE YANKEES PENETRATE THE SOUTHLAND

1. David D. Porter, report to Gideon Welles, Flagship *Black Hawk,* mouth of the Red River, May 16, 1864, in *ORN,* I, 26:130 (1914).

2. Jenkin Lloyd Jones, *An Artilleryman's Diary* (Madison, Wisc.: Wisconsin History Commission, 1914), 166–210; Theodore Upson, *With Sherman to the Sea: The Civil War Letters, Diaries, and Reminiscences of Theodore F. Upson,* ed. Oscar Osburn Winther (Baton Rouge: Louisiana State University Press, 1943), 102–105.

3. Lee, *Wartime Papers,* 659–60; Mary A. H. Gay, *Life in Dixie during the War, 1863–1864–1865,* 3d ed. (Atlanta: Constitution Job Office, 1892), 79–86.

4. Grant, *Papers,* X, 273–75.

5. Lee, *Wartime Papers,* 719.

6. J. Harvie Dew, "The Yankee and Rebel Yells," *Century Illustrated* 43 (April 1892): 954.

7. Martin T. McMahon, "The Death of General Sedgwick," *Battles and Leaders,* ed. Johnson and Buel, IV, 175; Augustus C. Brown, *The Diary of a Line Officer* (New York: published by the author, 1906), 43–44.

8. Grant, *Papers,* X, 422; Ezra J. Warner, *Generals in Gray: Lives of the Confederate Commanders* (Baton Rouge: Louisiana State University Press, 1959), 235.

9. Charles S. Venable, "General Lee in the Wilderness Campaign," *Battles and Leaders,* ed. Johnson and Buel, IV, 245; Peter S. Michie, *The Life and Letters of Emory Upton, Colonel of the Fourth Regiment of Artillery, and Brevet Major-General, U.S. Army* (New York: D. Appleton, 1885), 108; Richard Corbin, "Letters of a Confederate Officer to His Family in Europe during the Last Year of the War for Secession," *Magazine of History,* Extra No. 24 (1913): 23.

10. Brown, *Diary of a Line Officer,* 77–82.

11. John Chipman Gray and John Codman Ropes, *War Letters, 1862–1865, of John Chipman Gray and John Codman Ropes,* ed. Worthington Chauncey Ford (Boston: Houghton Mifflin, 1927), 364–66.

12. William T. Sherman, *Memoirs of General W. T. Sherman: Written by Himself,* ed. M. A. DeWolfe Howe (New York: D. Appleton, 1875), II, 125–27.

13. J. William Jones, *Life and Letters of Gen. Robert E. Lee* (New York: Neale, 1906), 306.

14. Charles Lee Lewis, *David Glasgow Farragut* (Annapolis, Md.: United States Naval Institute, 1941–1943), II, 269.

15. Lincoln, *Collected Works,* VIII, 11; Henry Steele Commager, ed., *The Blue and the Gray: The Story of the Civil War As Told by Participants* (Indianapolis: Bobbs-Merrill, 1950), 1048; Walter H. Taylor, *Lee's Adjutant: The Wartime Letters of Colonel Walter Herron Taylor, 1862–1865,* ed. R. Lockwood Tower (Columbia, S.C.: University of South Carolina Press, 1995), 190–91.

16. Wiley Britton, "Resumé of Military Operations in Arkansas and Missouri, 1864–1865," *Battles and Leaders,* ed. Johnson and Buel, IV, 376.

17. Philip H. Sheridan, report to Ulysses S. Grant, Woodstock, Va., October 7, 1864, in *OR,* XLIII:I, 30.

18. Small, *Road to Richmond,* 171–76; Marcus B. Toney, *The Privations of a Private: The Campaign under Gen. R. E. Lee, the Campaign under Gen. Stonewall Jackson, Bragg's Invasion of Kentucky, the Chickamauga Campaign, Prison Life in the North* (Nashville: published by the author, 1905), 93–104; John W. Headley, *Confederate Operations in Canada and New York* (New York: Neale, 1906), 274–77.

19. George Ward Nichols, *The Story of the Great March, from the Diary of a Staff Officer* (New York: Harper and Bros., 1865), 48–55.

20. James H. Wilson, *Under the Old Flag: Recollections of Military Operations in the War for the Union, the Spanish War, the Boxer Rebellion, etc.* (New York: D. Appleton, 1912), II, 99–121.

21. Gray, in the field near Savannah, December 14, 1864, *Proceedings of the Massachusetts Historical Society,* 49 (1915–1916): 393–94.

"WE ARE ALL COMRADES AGAIN"

1. Howell Cobb, letter to James A. Seddon, Richmond, January 8, 1865, in *OR,* IV:III, 1009.

2. Sherman, *Home Letters,* 324–27.

3. Eliza Andrews, *The War-Time Journal of a Georgia Girl, 1864–1865* (New York: D. Appleton, 1908), 76–79.

4. Augustus C. Buell, *"The Cannoneer": Recollections of Service in the Army of the Potomac, by "a Detached Volunteer" in the Regular Artillery* (Washington, D.C.: National Tribune, 1890), 328–33.

5. Lee, *Wartime Papers,* 329–30.

6. Jones, *Rebel War Clerk's Diary,* II, 418.

7. George D. Harmon, ed., "Letters of Luther Rice Mills: A Confederate Soldier," *North Carolina Historical Review* 4 (July 1927): 303; Josiah Gorgas, *The Journals of Josiah Gorgas, 1857–1878* (Tuscaloosa: University of Alabama Press, 1995), 153–54.

8. Lincoln, *Collected Works,* 332–33.

9. Peter S. Carmichael, *Lee's Young Artillerist: William R. J. Pegram* (Charlottesville: University Press of Virginia, 1995), 163.

10. Constance Cary Harrison, *Recollections Grave and Gay* (New York: Charles Scribner's Sons, 1911), 211.

11. Nichols, *Story of the Great March,* 160–66.

12. John Sergeant Wise, *The End of an Era* (Boston: Houghton Mifflin, 1902), 434; Lincoln, *Collected Works,* VIII, 392.

13. Joshua L. Chamberlain, *The Passing of the Armies: An Account of the Final Campaign of the Army of the Potomac, based upon Personal Reminiscences of the Fifth Army Corps* (New York: G. P. Putnam's Sons, 1915), 242; Horace Porter, "The Surrender at Appomattox Court House," *Battles and Leaders,* ed. Johnson and Buel, IV, 737.

14. Porter, "Surrender at Appomattox Court House," 743; Robert E. Lee, General Order No. 9, Appomattox Court House, Va., April 9, 1865, in *Wartime Papers,* 934–35; Catherine Ann Devereux Edmondston, *"Journal of a Secesh Lady": The Diary of Catherine Ann Devereux Edmondston,* ed. Beth Gilbert Crabtree and James W. Patton (Raleigh: North Carolina Division of Archives and History, 1979), 694–95.

15. Mary Cadwalader Jones, *Lantern Slides* (Boston: Published by the author, 1937) [not paginated].

16. Gideon Welles, *The Diary of Gideon Welles* (Boston: Houghton Mifflin, 1911), 286–87.

17. Edmund Ruffin, *The Diary of Edmund Ruffin* (Baton Rouge: Louisiana State University Press, 1972–1989), III, 949.

18. Walt Whitman, *Memoranda during the War* (Camden, N.J.: Published by the author, 1875–1876), 5.

19. Ambrose Bierce, "A Bivouac of the Dead," in *The Civil War Short Stories of Ambrose Bierce,* ed. Ernest J. Hopkins (New York: Doubleday, 1970), 139.

BIBLIOGRAPHY

Abell, Sam, and Brian C. Pohanka. *The Civil War: An Aerial Portrait.* Charlottesville, Va., 1990.

———. *Distant Thunder: A Photographic Essay on the American Civil War.* Charlottesville, Va., 1988.

Andrews, Eliza Frances. *The War-Time Journal of a Georgia Girl, 1864–1865.* New York, 1908.

Bierce, Ambrose. *The Civil War Short Stories of Ambrose Bierce.* Edited by Ernest J. Hopkins. New York, 1970.

Billings, John D. *Hardtack and Coffee; or, the Unwritten Story of Army Life, including Chapters on Enlisting, Life in Tents and Log Huts, Jonahs and Beats, Offences and Punishments, Raw Recruits, Foraging, Corps and Corps Badges, the Wagon Trains, the Army Mule, the Engineer Corps, etc.* Boston, 1887.

Blackford, Charles Minor. *Memoirs of Life in and out of the Army in Virginia during the War between the States.* Edited by Susan Leigh Colston Blackford. Lynchburg, Va., 1894–1896.

Blight, David W. *Frederick Douglass' Civil War: Keeping Faith in Jubilee.* Baton Rouge, 1989.

Borcke, Johann August Heinrich Heros von. *Memoirs of the Confederate War for Independence.* Edinburgh, 1866.

Brooks, Noah. *Washington in Lincoln's Time.* New York, 1895.

Brown, Augustus C. *The Diary of a Line Officer.* New York, 1906.

Buell, Augustus C. *"The Cannoneer": Recollections of Service in the Army of the Potomac, by "a Detached Volunteer" in the Regular Artillery.* Washington, D.C., 1890.

Carmichael, Peter S. *Lee's Young Artillerist: William R. J. Pegram.* Charlottesville, Va., 1995.

Chamberlain, Joshua L. *The Passing of the Armies: An Account of the Final Campaign of* the Army of the Potomac, based upon Personal Reminiscences of the Fifth Army Corps. New York, 1915.

Chesnut, Mary Boykin. *Mary Chesnut's Civil War.* Edited by C. Vann Woodward. New Haven, Conn., 1981.

Commager, Henry Steele, ed. *The Blue and the Gray: The Story of the Civil War As Told by Participants.* Indianapolis, 1950.

Connolly, James A. "Major Connolly's Letters to His Wife, 1862–1865." *Transactions of the Illinois State Historical Society for the Year 1928.* Springfield, Ill., 1928.

Cooke, John Esten. *Wearing of the Gray, being Personal Portraits, Scenes, and Adventures of the War.* Baltimore, 1867.

Cumming, Kate. *Gleanings from Southland: Sketches of Life and Manners of the People of the South before, during, and after the War of Secession.* Birmingham, Ala., 1895.

Dabney, Robert L. *Life and Campaigns of Lieut.-Gen. Thomas J. Jackson (Stonewall Jackson).* London, 1864–1866.

Davis, Charles E. Jr. *Three Years in the Army: The Story of the Thirteenth Massachusetts Volunteers, from July 16, 1861, to August 1, 1864.* Boston, 1894.

Davis, Jefferson Finis. *The Papers of Jefferson Davis.* Edited by Haskell M. Monroe Jr., James T. McIntosh, Lynda Lasswell Crist, Mary Seaton Dix, Richard E. Beringer, and Kenneth H. Williams. 9 vols. to date. Baton Rouge, 1971–1997.

Day, Samuel Phillips. *Down South; or, an Englishman's Experience at the Seat of the American War.* London, 1862.

DeLeon, Thomas Cooper. *Four Years in Rebel Capitals: An Inside View of Life in the Southern Confederacy, from Birth to Death, from Original Notes, Collated in the Years 1861 to 1865.* Mobile, Ala., 1890.

Dwight, Wilder. *The Life and Letters of Wilder Dwight, Lieut.-Col. Second Mass. Inf. Vols.* Boston, 1868.

Early, Jubal A., J. William Jones, Robert A. Brock, James P. Smith, Hamilton J. Eckenrode, Douglas Southall Freeman, and Frank E. Vandiver, eds. *Southern Historical Society Papers.* 52 vols. Richmond, 1876–1959.

Edmondston, Catherine Ann Devereux. *"Journal of a Secesh Lady": The Diary of Catherine Ann Devereux Edmondston.* Edited by Beth Gilbert Crabtree and James W. Patton. Raleigh, N.C., 1979.

Eicher, David J. *Civil War Battlefields: A Touring Guide.* Dallas, 1995.

———. *The Civil War in Books: An Analytical Bibliography.* Urbana, Ill., 1996.

———. *Robert E. Lee: A Life Portrait.* Dallas, 1997.

Fitch, Michael H. *Echoes of the Civil War As I Hear Them.* New York, 1905.

Gay, Mary Ann Harris. *Life in Dixie during the War, 1863–1864–1865.* Atlanta, 1892.

Gerrish, Theodore. *Army Life: A Private's Reminiscences of the Civil War.* Portland, Maine, 1882.

Gordon, John B. *Reminiscences of the Civil War.* New York, 1903.

Gorgas, Josiah. *The Journals of Josiah Gorgas, 1857–1878.* Edited by Sarah Woolfolk Wiggins. Tuscaloosa, Ala., 1995.

Grant, Ulysses S. *The Papers of Ulysses S. Grant.* Edited by John Y. Simon. 20 vols. to date. Carbondale, 1967–1995.

———. *Personal Memoirs of U. S. Grant.* New York, 1885–1886.

Gray, John Chipman, and John Codman Ropes. *War Letters, 1862–1865, of John Chipman Gray and John Codman Ropes.* Edited by Worthington Chauncey Ford. Boston, 1927.

Harrison, Constance Cary. *Recollections Grave and Gay.* New York, 1911.

Haskell, Frank Aretas. *Haskell of Gettysburg: His Life and Civil War Papers.* Madison, Wisc., 1970.

Haupt, Herman. *Reminiscences of General Herman Haupt: Giving Hitherto Unpublished Official Orders, Personal Narratives of Important Military Operations, and Interviews with President Lincoln, Secretary Stanton, General-in-Chief Halleck, and with Generals McDowell, McClellan, Meade, Hancock, Burnside, and Others in Command of the Armies in the Field, and His Impressions of These Men.* Milwaukee, 1901.

Headley, John W. *Confederate Operations in Canada and New York.* New York, 1906.

Hedley, Fenwick Y. *Marching through Georgia: Pen Pictures of Every-Day Life in General Sherman's Army, from the Beginning of the Atlanta Campaign until the Close of the War.* Chicago, 1885.

Hood, John Bell. *Advance and Retreat: Personal Experiences in the United States and Confederate States Armies.* New Orleans, 1880.

Hunter, Alexander. *Johnny Reb and Billy Yank.* New York, 1905.

Jackson, Mary Anna. *Life and Letters of General Thomas J. Jackson (Stonewall Jackson).* New York, 1892.

Jackson, Oscar L. *The Colonel's Diary: Journals Kept before and during the Civil War, by the Late Colonel Oscar L. Jackson of New Castle, Pennsylvania, Sometime Commander of the 63d Regiment O.V.I.* Sharon, Pa., 1922.

Johnson, Charles F. *The Long Roll, being a Journal of the Civil War, as set down during the years 1861–1863.* East Aurora, N.Y., 1911.

Johnson, Robert Underwood, and Clarence Clough Buel, eds. *Battles and Leaders of the Civil War, Being for the Most Part Contributions by Union and Confederate Officers: Based upon "The Century" War Series.* New York, 1887–1888.

Jones, J. William. *Life and Letters of Gen. Robert E. Lee.* New York, 1906.

Jones, Jenkin Lloyd. *An Artilleryman's Diary.* Madison, Wisc., 1914.

Jones, John B. *A Rebel War Clerk's Diary at the Confederate States Capital.* Philadelphia, 1866.

Jones, Mary Cadwalader. *Lantern Slides.* Published by the author, Boston, 1937.

King, W. C., and W. P. Derby, eds. *Camp-Fire Sketches and Battle-Field Echoes of '61–5.* Springfield, Mass., 1887.

Lawrence, Eugene. "Grant on the Battle-Field." *Harper's New Monthly* 39 (1869): 212.

Lee, Robert E. *The Wartime Papers of R. E. Lee.* Edited by Clifford Dowdey and Louis H. Manarin. Boston, 1961.

Lee, Robert E. Jr. *Recollections and Letters of General Robert E. Lee.* New York, 1904.

LeGrand, Julia. *The Journal of Julia LeGrand: New Orleans, 1862–1863.* Edited by Kate Mason Rowland and Mrs. Morris L. Croxall. Richmond, 1911.

Lewis, Charles Lee. *David Glasgow Farragut.* Annapolis, Md., 1941–1943.

Lincoln, Abraham. *The Collected Works of Abraham Lincoln.* Edited by Roy P. Basler. 11 vols. New Brunswick, N.J., 1953–1955, Westport, Conn., 1974, and New Brunswick, N.J., 1990.

Livermore, Thomas L. *Days and Events, 1860–1866.* Boston, 1920.

Longstreet, James. *From Manassas to Appomattox: Memoirs of the Civil War in America.* Philadelphia, 1896.

Lusk, William Thompson. *War Letters of William Thompson Lusk, Captain, Assistant Adjutant-General United States Volunteers, 1861–1863.* New York, 1911.

Masur, Louis P., ed. *The Real War Will Never Get in the Books: Selections from Writers during the Civil War.* New York, 1993.

McCarthy, Carlton. *Detailed Minutiae of Soldier Life in the Army of Northern Virginia, 1861–1865.* Richmond, 1882.

McClellan, George B. *The Civil War Papers of George B. McClellan: Selected Correspondence, 1860–1865.* Edited by Stephen W. Sears. New York, 1989.

McClure, Alexander K., ed. *The Annals of the War Written by Leading Participants North and South: Originally Published in the* Philadelphia Weekly Times. Philadelphia, 1879.

Michie, Peter S. *The Life and Letters of Emory Upton, Colonel of the Fourth Regiment of Artillery, and Brevet Major-General, U.S. Army.* New York, 1885.

[Military Order of the Loyal Legion of the United States]. *Papers of the Military Order of the Loyal Legion of the United States, 1887–1915.* Wilmington, N.C., 1991–1996.

Moore, Frank, ed. *The Rebellion Record: A Diary of American Events, with Documents, Narratives, Illustrative Incidents, Poetry, etc.* New York, 1861–180.

Muench, David, and Michael B. Ballard. *Landscapes of Battle: The Civil War.* Jackson, Miss., 1988.

Nichols, George Ward. *The Story of the Great March, from the Diary of a Staff Officer.* New York, 1865.

Norton, Oliver W. *Army Letters, 1861–1865, being Extracts from Private Letters to Relatives and Friends from a Soldier in the Field during the Late Civil War, with an Appendix Containing Copies of Some Official Documents, Papers, and Addresses of a Later Date.* Chicago, 1903.

Oates, Stephen B. *To Purge This Land with Blood: A Biography of John Brown.* New York, 1970.

Owen, William Miller. *In Camp and Battle with the Washington Artillery of New Orleans: A Narrative of Events during the Late Civil War from Bull Run to Appomattox and Spanish Fort.* Boston, 1885.

Pease, William H., and Jane H. Pease. *James Louis Petigru: Southern Conservative, Southern Dissenter.* Athens, Ga., 1995.

Polley, Joseph B. *A Soldier's Letters to Charming Nellie.* New York, 1908.

Rice, Allen Thorndike, ed. "A Page of Political Correspondence: Unpublished Letters of Mr. Stanton to Mr. Buchanan." *North American Review* 129 (1879): 482.

Ropes, John Codman, and Theodore F. Dwight, eds. *Papers of the Military Historical Society of Massachusetts.* Wilmington, N.C., 1990.

Ruffin, Edmund. *The Diary of Edmund Ruffin.* Edited by William K. Scarborough. 3 vols. Baton Rouge, 1972–1989.

Russell, William Howard. *My Diary North and South.* New York, 1954.

Sandburg, Carl. *Abraham Lincoln: The War Years.* 4 vols. New York, 1939.

Sears, Stephen W. *George B. McClellan: The Young Napoleon.* New York, 1988.

Sherman, William Tecumseh. *Home Letters of General Sherman*. New York, 1909.

———. *Memoirs of General W. T. Sherman: Written by Himself.* Edited by M. A. DeWolfe Howe. New York, 1875.

Shotwell, Randolph Abbott. *The Papers of Randolph Abbott Shotwell*. Edited by J. G. Roulhac Hamilton. Raleigh, N.C., 1929–1936.

Small, Abner. *The Road to Richmond: The Civil War Memoirs of Major Abner R. Small of the Sixteenth Maine Volunteers, together with the Diary which he kept when he was a Prisoner of War.* Edited by Harold A. Small. Berkeley, Calif., 1939.

Stanley, Henry M. *The Autobiography of Sir Henry Morton Stanley.* Edited by Dorothy Stanley. New York, 1909.

Stiles, Robert. *Four Years under Marse Robert.* New York, 1903.

Stillwell, Leander. *The Story of a Common Soldier of Army Life in the Civil War, 1861–1865.* Kansas City, Mo., 1920.

Strother, David Hunter. *A Virginia Yankee in the Civil War: The Diaries of David Hunter Strother.* Edited by Cecil D. Eby. Chapel Hill, N.C., 1961.

Taylor, Walter H. *Lee's Adjutant: The Wartime Letters of Colonel Walter Herron Taylor, 1862–1865.* Edited by R. Tower Lockwood. Columbia, S.C., 1995.

Toney, Marcus B. *The Privations of a Private: The Campaign under Gen. R. E. Lee, the Campaign under Gen. Stonewall Jackson, Bragg's Invasion of Kentucky, the Chickamauga Campaign, Prison Life in the North.* Nashville, 1905.

Tyler, Lyon G., ed. *The Letters and Times of the Tylers.* New York, 1970.

Upson, Theodore. *With Sherman to the Sea: The Civil War Letters, Diaries, and Reminiscences of Theodore F. Upson.* Edited by Oscar Osburn Winther. Baton Rouge, 1943.

[U.S. Navy Department]. *Official Records of the Union and Confederate Navies in the War of the Rebellion.* 31 vols. Washington, D.C., 1894–1927.

[U.S. War Department]. *The War of the Rebellion: A Compilation of the Official Records of the Union and Confederate Armies.* 128 vols. Washington, D.C., 1880–1901.

Warner, Ezra J. *Generals in Gray: Lives of the Confederate Commanders.* Baton Rouge, 1959.

Watson, William. *Life in the Confederate Army, being the Observations and Experiences of an Alien in the South during the American Civil War.* London, 1887.

Welles, Gideon. *The Diary of Gideon Welles.* Boston, 1911.

Whitman, Walt. *Memoranda during the War.* Camden, N.J., 1875–1876.

Wilson, James H. *Under the Old Flag: Recollections of Military Operations in the War for the Union, the Spanish War, the Boxer Rebellion, etc.* New York, 1912.

Winthrop, Theodore. *Life in the Open Air, and Other Papers.* Boston, 1863.

Wise, John Sergeant. *The End of an Era.* Boston, 1902.

INDEX

Italic page numbers indicate photographs